© Copyright 2019 by

The right of J Smith to be identified as the sole author of this work

has been asserted by him in accordance with

the Copyright, Designs and Patents Act 1988.

First published 2019 by Railhead Publishing.

First Kindle edition published August, 2019.

Second Kindle edition published September, 2019.

First paperback edition published December, 2019.

The cover is courtesy of Pixabay. https://pixabay.com/

You may not copy, store, distribute, transmit, reproduce
or

otherwise make available this publication (or any part of it)

in any form, or by any means (electronic, digital, optical,

mechanical, photocopying, recording or otherwise), without

the prior written permission of the publisher. Any person

who does any unauthorised act in relation to this

publication may be liable to criminal prosecution

and civil claims for damages.

What Do Train Drivers Do?

A Day In The Life Of A Driver

by J Smith

Railhead Publishing

Contents

Introduction

1   Getting Up

2   Getting To Work

3   At The Depot

4   Preparing The Train/Getting Onboard

5   Depot To Station

6   At The Station

7   Let's Talk About Training

8   Driving Part 1

9   Arriving Part 1

10   Driving Part 2

11   Arriving Part 2

12   Back To The Depot

13   End of Shift

14   Home

Afterword

Foreword

As an ex-Train Driver (or Engineer or Engineman or Motorman or whatever they call them in your country) I wanted to write this to give people some idea of what being a Train Driver is like.

There don't seem to be many books around that describe in detail what it's like to drive trains and live that life. I see internet comments which are sometimes critical of Train Drivers. This is often due to the fact that Drivers are now paid much higher salaries than they were in the past. Increasingly, rail companies realised that they wanted good people at the controls of these machines. The consequences of mistakes on the railway, particularly by Drivers, could be fatal. Sometimes dozens of people have died due to a Driver's error. It's an unusually responsible job and it's not for everyone.

It's also a job which takes a major toll on your personal life. Getting up at 2AM, and then being expected to still be fully conscious and concentrating intensely 10 hours later is a big ask. Drivers get it done but it's far from easy.

I want to take you through a day as a Train Driver. I hope you enjoy it, and that you come away from it with a better understanding of what Drivers go through. You'll frequently find sentences beginning 'IN THE OLD DAYS'. This is because it's often enlightening to recall changes which have led to the present day industry.

However, this has been done so often that I thought it best to flag it, otherwise you'll think I'm an old blowhard. The text is also interspersed with mini-sections on sub-topics, to break up the 'diary of a day' format and hopefully provide more detailed and interesting information. These are "Things That Can Happen While You're Driving A Train", "Only On The Railway?" and "Railway Matters".

Terminology. This is a tough one. I've tried to keep things comprehensible, but after many years in the industry I have a tendency to use different terms for the same thing – just like every other Driver. 'Vehicle', 'coach' and 'car' is a good example. These can all refer to a single 'vehicle' on a Passenger train. I didn't want to include a Glossary as that just makes things more of a chore for the reader, so I hope I've explained things with enough clarity.

I will be mentioning the same topics in several different parts of the book. This is the nature of the beast. I've tried not to repeat myself too blatantly, but if you get an occasional sense of déjà vu then I can only apologise.

So…Train Driving. It's a tough job but also enjoyable. A lot of good people have given their entire working lives to the rail industry. And some have given their actual lives while working in it. I hope this book gives you some idea of what it takes to do the job day in and day out.

As an ex-Driver there may well be details and technicalities which have changed since my employment. I can only describe things as they were when I did the job, or as they were related to me at that particular time. This book is not intended to describe accurately what any country's rail industry is like today, but is simply one person's impressions from the past. I sincerely hope you enjoy it.

PLEASE NOTE : I'm pleased to say there are many more lady Drivers in the industry than when I began my career. Please understand that when I'm talking about Drivers, this could be a lady just as easily as it could be a man. There are also transgender employees in the rail industry, as everywhere else. All references to 'Driver' or 'Drivers' should be taken to refer to anyone who performs that role.

J Smith,

July, 2019.

1

Getting Up

So let's pretend you're a Train Driver.

Life is about tootling along on your locomotive, waving at friendly farmers and smiling kids, earning a pretty sum…isn't it?

Let's take a closer look.

It's 2.15AM. Since you're pretending to be a Train Driver, you can start doing what they do, and use the 24-hour clock. That makes it 0215.

0215…Yes, you heard me. That time really does exist.

And for some unlucky people like Train Drivers, you may be required to be awake, and more importantly, functional.

The alarm has gone off and disturbed your wife/husband/partner/boyfriend/girlfriend/cat/dog/ailing relative/neighbours/burglars and who knows who else. Your brain is struggling with thoughts like '*What the hell is going on?*' and '*Getting up at crazy 'o clock should be illegal*' and '*Maybe I'm just dreaming*' and sometimes '*Just 5 more minutes…what harm could it do?*' This last thought is likely to get you fired. Because if you really do lie down again, even for a few seconds, your brain will likely hit the 'OFF' switch and you will oversleep and you will be late to work. Rail companies, funnily enough, don't like employees to sleep in, particularly Train Drivers. Also, try hitting 'Snooze' a few times at 0215 and see what that does for your personal relationships.

So, you actually get up.

At 0215.

The first major hurdle of your day as a Train Driver is successfully negotiated.

But, wait a minute. How exactly did you manage this?

Let's rewind to 1800 (6PM – get with it!) the previous day.

It's a glorious Summer evening. Friends and family are making the most of the good weather. You, on the other hand, having eaten 'dinner' around 1600/4PM (because eating dinner immediately before trying to get a full night's sleep in bright Summer daylight is NOT A GOOD IDEA) are going for a shower. You can either shower at 1800/6PM or, in a tired rush, at 0215. The 0215 shower might even help partially wake you up. Unfortunately, depending on your domestic arrangements, it might also help wake up other people.

You've just showered at 1800/6PM (because your plumbing can make strange noises, disturbing or indeed terrifying others at 0215) and now you're clean and raring to go! To bed…

With the world enjoying the sunshine, with friends and family doing enjoyable stuff, with your neighbours making all kinds of racket (how DARE they cut the grass/have a barbecue/have friends visit/etc. at 1830/6.30PM), with kids playing in the street, YOU are going to sleep.

If I'm giving you the impression this is a) difficult, and b) as enjoyable as a visit to the dentist for root canal, then you're getting the idea.

Face facts : you're not getting to sleep.

Particularly on the first night of a new shift rotation…it's just not going to happen. I've heard of Drivers finishing a week of afternoon shifts (can be called 'backshifts' or 'lates' or similar) on a Friday evening. So their biological clocks have just gotten attuned to that rhythm. And they then have Saturday and Sunday supposedly 'off' work before getting up at 0215 Monday morning. Those people will be lucky if they get as much as 3 hours' sleep that first night…sometimes they get none at all.

On subsequent days they will become so horrendously tired that they will eventually get a longer sleep (assuming they don't have neighbours who selfishly, you know, DO stuff in the evenings. In which case it may be the 4th or 5th night before extreme exhaustion allows prolonged sleep – at the risk of sleeping in, of course.) And remember, after 4 or 5 consecutive days of this nightmare, your shift changes again.

You may as well take a hammer to your biological clock. I can't imagine why shift workers have higher levels of cancer, heart disease and other major health issues. What on earth could be causing this? (I just choked on my own sarcasm.)

"Railway Matters"

Okay. Let's get this one out of the way right at the start. The answer to the question "Do Train Drivers have to steer the train?" is a definite "No". We have controls for power – we make it move. And we have controls for brakes – we make it stop. When I used to explain this to anyone who'd asked, they'd often reply something like "That makes things a lot easier for you then, doesn't it?" To which I wanted to say "Yes, of course. Stopping nine coaches weighing around 400 tonnes, from 125mph, in torrential rain and cold temperatures, during darkness...is so easy. A child could do it."

Of course, I'm being a bit harsh here – the general public has very little idea of the numerous challenges involved in driving trains, which is partly why I wanted to write this book. There are plenty of controls and dials and gauges and warning lights in the cab of a train, all of which we keep a close eye on. And knowing where and how to brake, as you approach a station or freight yard in all weathers and times of day, is a major part of a Driver's skill. But the basic position is that we apply power or we apply brakes. We can also coast along, obviously...

This lack of any steering requirement didn't stop many Drivers through the years, when they had some cab visitor with no railway knowledge, and one of the old locomotives with a round wheel on the non-Driver side (which was for applying the parking brake when the loco was shut down), requesting that the visitor 'steer' the train with the wheel on their side of the cab. After goodness knows how many minutes of white-knuckle stress for the poor visitor, and much suppressed chuckling by the other cab occupants, the hapless person would be told that they were turning a parking brake and that it was not actually doing anything. And no, I didn't do that to anyone!

Back to sleeping, and of course, Train Drivers do sometimes resort to 'outside help' for getting to sleep. IN THE OLD DAYS alcohol was used – and during the day too! Some people try to stick to a rigid, pre-bed routine. Some people order things off the internet (that don't contravene regulations). Some claim to just 'tough it out'. There's a full spectrum of approaches, but not always a willingness to talk about it. Rail is a macho industry (we may come back to that…)

Here's the thing: unless you've done something like what I'm describing (get up at crazy 'o clock for multiple nights, then switch soon after to an opposite routine and repeat these swings indefinitely) YOU HAVE NO CLUE WHAT IT'S REALLY LIKE. Drivers hear the same thing from countless relatives/friends/strangers : *"You get up at 2.15AM? That must be hard."* And they skip off back to their 9-5, Monday to Friday existences and, man, THEY HAVE NO CLUE. Even people who are 'shift workers' tend to have a solid rota, one of the most common being 6AM-2PM, 2PM-10PM, 10PM-

6AM. The hours worked by Train Drivers are peculiar and spectacular. And stink.

It varies from company to company, and even within companies at different locations, but Drivers may not even do the same shift for a working week. I've heard of depots where they work a different shift every single day. This isn't such a big deal on backshifts in the afternoons, or dayshifts, but if you're on early shifts then working a week with shifts at 0345 then 0430 then 0500 then 0355 will REALLY mess with your body clock.

And unlike many other shift workers, Train Drivers can't sneak a quick nap when they feel like it. In fact, legally speaking, Train Drivers are supposed to be just as awake driving a 1000 tonne freight train or several hundred passengers at 100mph in the middle of the night, as they would be in the middle of the day. If you screw up and cause significant damage and disruption, or even deaths, the Police don't say *"Well it was 3AM and the Driver was only 75% awake so we'll prosecute him 25% less"*. Did I mention it's a responsible job? How many jobs are there where each working day you can make a mistake and kill dozens of people? It's a pretty short list.

Getting back to the macho industry...Older Drivers in particular don't think they should complain about 'fatigue'. There's a bizarre attitude of 'Well it was even harder in the past.' They don't always like it when young Drivers ask 'Does it really need to be this hard?' There are a few Clint Eastwoods around. *"Did I put five cups of tea in this flask or four? Well, punk? Do you feel lucky?"* Etc.

So let's get back to 0215. You'll enjoy shaving while half asleep. Or trying to apply makeup effectively if you're a lady. You drag on your clothes (hopefully the right way around) which you've professionally prepared the night before (or, if you're lucky, your wife/partner may have done it). Let me say this : all good Drivers have neat uniforms. It's a built-in part of the whole professional package. Hey, neat Drivers can screw up on the job too. I just think they're less likely to if that neatness is part of an overall 'professional' approach to the role – as it should be.

There's a spectrum of uniforms too. Freight companies are more relaxed about this (the evidence is on every station platform), and maybe they should be as the hours on Freight are generally much worse. Passenger companies are understandably stricter – you may be getting up at 0215 but you may well find yourself on display to the public at a busy station platform 10 hours later, possibly with grumpy members of the public trying to find out why their fantastically expensive seat on the 1200 to Wherever has just vanished due to last-minute cancellation.

"Railway Matters"

Let's not beat around the bush. If you become a Train Driver, unless you're in one of the very rare companies who follow rigid working hours and have most weekends off, your personal life will be totally transformed. You are rightly expected to treat the job as a serious profession. This means putting a lot of effort into getting enough sleep (as we've seen, no easy feat), into not drinking and being careful with medicines (you don't need to give up drinking but it cannot happen anywhere near a Driving shift), and to ensuring you keep up to date with all rules and procedures (not as easy as it sounds if you do it properly).

In addition you will be required to wear a uniform and look the part of a person charged with the responsibility of transporting hundreds of lives (at possibly high speed) on a regular basis. Your company may also ask you to change the shift you're supposed to work the following day, or work on your day off – none of that is compulsory but it will be asked.

All of these things require effort on your part, and will impact enormously on your personal relationships and leisure time. Your life will change substantially. The majority of people either take these things in their stride – although that's a lot easier the younger you are – or make the necessary changes to take their new career seriously.

Unfortunately there are those who either quit or don't make the necessary changes. I know of several people who quit, usually fairly early in the training or, more commonly, in the first six months after training. The lifestyle required can be quite a shock for some people, particularly those who prize their social life above all else. The ones who stay in the job but simply don't take it seriously enough will find their disciplinary records earning them a place out the door, sooner or later. It's a big commitment, it's not for everyone, but it can be a damn good job for the right person.

Most Drivers go to work on these very early shifts without eating – your stomach is at least as confused as the rest of your body as to what the hell you're doing getting up at this time of day, and doesn't need any extra aggravation. There are some Drivers who do force food down in an effort to either wake up, or provide the fuel to wake up fully a little later on. Many Drivers don't even drink coffee before leaving the house, preferring to get it upon arriving at work. I always had a strong cup before going anywhere – you'll still be in plenty trouble if you crash your car on the way to work due to not being alert. Not everyone perks up with caffeine though, and there's a big spectrum regarding what people eat or drink in the middle of the night.

If you're lucky you'll be going into the refrigerator to retrieve whatever's been made for you as 'lunch', to be eaten at some later time (if you get up at 0215, your 'lunchtime' should be around 0830 or 0900.) Making your own rolls/sandwiches/salads/anything appetising at 0245 is not a pleasant or usually productive task. Neither is polishing company-issue footwear. Basically, on horror-level early shifts, everything should be readied the night before.

Do you know the only sensible, productive thing you can do at 0245? Go back to bed. You're not doing that because you're a professional Train Driver.

2

Getting To Work

You didn't sleep in. You're washed and dressed. Well done.

You now have your bag or rucksack with rolls/sandwiches/Nachos/steak/whatever plus a bottle of water/soda/energy drink/etc. Some guys take energy drinks or flasks of coffee to be drunk throughout the shift. Some people refuse to touch these 'wakefulness helpers'. I found coffee a huge help on earlies, but you had to keep drinking it or there was a noticeable crash when the effects wore off.

You read the note/text from your partner warning you about some future social event that you're supposed to try and attend, and enter it in your diary (rail unions have a habit of handing out embossed diaries – these are actually very useful, although many people do diary 'business' on their phones these days.) There will now begin a potentially prolonged game of 'Can I Make This Event?' – this will include blind luck/shift-swapping/begging for leave, or a combination of all of these.

"Things That Can Happen While You're Driving A Train"

High winds are pretty nasty for Train Drivers. Aside from the indirect chaos caused to all electric trains if overhead electrification equipment is damaged, every train is a possible victim of the fallen tree. These rarely, if ever, actually fall on top of a train, but cause more than enough terror if you're driving a train at any kind of speed and round a curve to see a large one right across your track. It's in the lap of the Gods at that point. Some damage will be inevitable, dependent on what exactly you're driving and how fast you're travelling. Best case scenario is damage to the exterior at the front, but nothing which affects your onward progress. More serious scenarios might involve damage which requires certain equipment to be isolated out of use and speed restrictions imposed. Worst case is that the train is damaged to a level which makes it impossible to continue, and even possible injury to the Driver. It's no fun to have large pieces of tree coming through your windscreen with an accompaniment of high-velocity broken glass.

Of course, if the winds have been forecast correctly or detected in real time, trains will be cautioned. This means you will be told at a station stop, through a general radio broadcast, or stopped at a signal, and ordered to proceed at reduced speed for a certain period of time. Even then, things can go wrong. As mentioned elsewhere, trackside materials and equipment can become unexpected obstacles if not secured. If the speed you've been cautioned down to is still fast enough, you won't necessarily stop in time. Let's just say high winds are another tick in the 'Con' column. There, we got through a whole section on wind without mentioning farts. Ah nuts...I just did, didn't I?

Now you can leave the house. If you live in a city you may see milk being delivered or taxis depositing people – those with a normal job - who have had a fun night out, but chances are you're likely to feel you're in a science fiction film about the apocalypse…Not only is no-one around, not only are no vehicles moving, but it's eerily quiet.

As a Train Driver you will almost certainly have a car – most job advertisements for the last 15 to 20 years insist on it. I've heard of a few Drivers who didn't own cars. They either lived close enough to walk to work, or took their chances with night-time buses and taxis (rail companies are supremely underwhelmed to find a Driver who hasn't bought his own car delaying a train, with the excuse of "My taxi was late!")

So, unlike most of the rest of the world who will wake at 0600 or 0700, and have minor problems getting into work - in Winter for example, you have the dubious honour of being a 'pathfinder'. In Winter, you may well be the first car driver out there. The guys 10 feet up in their snowplough are squinting into the cold, foggy distance…"Who's that idiot?" Ho, ho. That's you! Not so groggy all of a sudden. Not after nearly wrapping your car around that streetlight after going sideways in the snow...

Of course, were we talking about a shift starting later in the day, then you might well use public transport to get to work. Even if you always require taking the car, starting later in the day removes a whole host of potential problems from your journey. Although it might also add a few, such as rush-hour traffic.

"Only On The Railway?"

A big part of being a Freight Driver – at least on a mixed-use track - involves sitting in a loop or siding, waiting for faster trains to pass you. Sometimes several are allowed to pass before you get going again. This is just part of the job. While it does give you a respite from driving for a while, it can become boring quite quickly unless you get into a routine.

Some Drivers use this as an opportunity to revise their manuals or operations notices. Others will simply read a newspaper, magazine or book. One eye must always be kept on the signal at the end of your loop or siding...you really don't want to be reading about the new cars being released next month, while the Signaller is waiting for you to get your train on the move before the next express gets there.

Of course, this is also a chance to answer the call of nature. Although some care has to be taken. You're not going to do that if your loop has a nice house located just beside your engine. Or if there's a motorway/highway/major road alongside. Having said that, you could be trapped in your cab for many hours, particularly if there is disruption on the railway. You may be choosing between peeing in an empty plastic bottle (which has been done by Drivers far more often than I care to think about) or someone seeing you peeing into a bush at the trackside. Yup, it's a strange job alright.

Back at crazy o'clock…and should you make it to your workplace in one piece (I had many scares in bad weather over the years but managed to never actually crash), you will often be borderline late due to the hazardous journey – and this happens even when you allow lots of extra time due to weather. Depending on your workplace, you may also have to negotiate some manner of grumpy and/or sleeping security guard, who may be manning a security gate/door which malfunctions in cold weather. Eventually you will reach the car park, and if your car door hasn't frozen shut (just when you thought the stress-filled journey was over) then you may actually have made it to work.

3

At The Depot

Congratulations!

You didn't : a) have the car not start at 0300, b) find part of the route to work closed for 'maintenance', requiring a lengthy diversion, or c) crash the car due to not being fully awake/weather.

You've arrived at work.

Depending on who you work for, you are now either at a large, closed station which will require entry via a security gate/door, or at a 'depot.' Depots vary considerably but are all based on a template from the days of 'old railways.' This usually means they are a grimy collection of functional buildings located either on waste ground or an industrial estate.

It's fair to say railway depots have zero concern for being in any way pleasing to the eye, or 'nice' places to work. They also tend to have a 'zoological' quality – over the years, at different depots, I've been up close and personal with foxes, squirrels, weasels, cats, stray dogs and rats. Many of them are attracted to depots by 'roadkill' or pieces of dead meat carried in on trains. Birds, sheep, stags, cats, dogs, occasionally cows but hopefully not humans (more on that later) can be transported for hundreds of miles if wedged appropriately on the underside of trains – as they often are at speed. Sometimes the scavenging animals in depots have an aggressive vibe of 'What do you think you're doing here? Got a problem, buddy?' if you come across them. Personal tip : don't get in the way of a hungry fox in the dark.

"Railway Matters"

Train Drivers have always been able to transfer from one depot to another within a company, and in the modern industry between companies too. It's fair to say these transfers have none of the glamour of sports stars, though. Younger Drivers, with no domestic responsibilities, would often move to get driving experience as soon as possible, with a view to transferring again at some future point. This would either be back to their 'home' location or to the location they ideally want to be based. It was usually difficult to get your ideal location because whatever positive points were enticing you to go there were also enticing lots of other Drivers. In the latter part of my career, transfers had changed substantially due to private companies taking over many parts of the industry.

Transferring, once your application was accepted, was simply a matter of being given a date to turn up at your new location. You would then undertake much of the training which a Trainee Driver does after he has completed his basic Driver training – traction courses (if it's a small rural depot you may only have one type of train to learn, perhaps taking a week or two depending on existing qualifications, while a large urban depot might require training on three or more classes of traction) and route learning. During this several weeks of training you would get plenty of opportunity to meet your new colleagues and figure out how things were done at the new location.

Undergoing a transfer is no small matter, unless you are in a large city and simply transferring a few miles – though even then, if you're changing company it could be quite an upheaval. I heard several stories of people who transferred and became unhappy fairly quickly (either with the new city/town or the depot itself). The situation then was basically 'tough luck', and they had to wait a certain period (three years in many instances) before submitting another transfer request. The reason for the period of non-transfer is because the new depot or company you've transferred to has spent time and money training you at the new location, and needs a return on that investment.

Of course, some Drivers stayed until retirement at the depot they joined as an 18-year old, because they had such strong family ties there or they were simply happy where they were. Whatever your individual circumstances it's good to know that the opportunity exists to sample life elsewhere, and this is definitely another tick in the 'Pro' column when it comes to Train Driving as a profession.

You'll make your way to the Drivers' area. This is a collection of rooms – locker room, canteen or dining area or 'mess room', and an administration room (often containing a fax/photocopier and 'mail slots' for each

Driver). IN THE OLD DAYS, railway mess rooms were often crowded, 95-100% male, with a thick fog of cigarette smoke and the overpowering stink of fried food. If you listened carefully among the bawdy humour and curse words you could almost hear the arteries harden.

Smoking has been banned in many countries for some years now, and different rail companies put varying amounts of effort into degrimifying their traincrew areas. Sometimes this can be overdone and you find garishly decorated rooms with 'modern' but uncomfortable furniture, surrounded by 'motivational' pictures, either of inspiring subjects or vomit-inducing phrases like 'There's No "I" In Team' or 'All Hail Our Glorious Management' (okay, I may have exaggerated with the last one.)

You may find yourself the only person at work at 0335. Freight companies tend to have more staff around at night or early morning, although some long-distance passenger companies can have very early starts too. If there is actually anyone else around, there's a strong chance they're either catching a quick nap or they're awake and grumpy as a hungover bear with a kidney stone. Often your morning conversation anytime between 0200 and 0500 will go as follows :

YOU : Morning (if you're going to be more macho about it, you might start with "You look like crap.")

COLLEAGUE WHO WAS NAPPING : What shift/turn/trip/train are you on?

YOU : The 4.45.

COLLEAGUE : Lucky you.

At which point he will probably fart loudly and go immediately back to sleep. Or continue watching TV. Or continue reading a paper. Or a Kindle (Train Drivers can be much more cultured than you'd think. And less so.) Now that your heartwarming and uplifting interactions with your colleague are complete, you can start the serious business.

In many companies, 'starting work' involves either going to an office window and saying "Hi" to a supervisor or clerk, or, as is becoming more popular to save costs, telephoning either a person or a machine. Companies now often have just one 'Rostering' or 'Resources' office for the whole company, rather than individual offices in each significant geographical location. Sometimes it's an automated system where you don't even need to talk to a human. Whatever the case, you have now officially 'started work.'

Different companies have different procedures for what happens next, but most are some variation on the following :

1. Check for changes to the day's work. A 'work schedule' for each individual shift generally runs for several months or longer, but it can be altered at short notice or even on the day (usually 24 or 48hrs notice is given if possible, but they may ask you on the day.) Occasionally a Supervisor or Clerk will ask you to do something quite different from what you've come in to

do. This doesn't happen often and tends to involve major disruption (failed train blocking the line, flooding, broken rail, giant screaming mutant turkeys on the line – wait, that last one may have been a magnificent dream.) Let's take a look at an example of a work schedule.

Driver's Work Schedule/Turn/Trip/Shift

This is simply a list of what the Driver is required to do during the shift in question. These are laid out in a particular format, but for ease of explanation I'll just list the elements :

SH02, M-F, 0335-1100, 15/06-02/12. Traction, Headcode, Action, Dep, Arr.

Firstly, all rail companies use something along these lines, as they've been used in the industry since the year nineteen-oatcake. The details may differ, but this is basically the way Train Drivers know what they're supposed to be doing every day. These Schedules may be kept in a binder in the admin room, or if the company's embracing technology, on a company-issue tablet (if so, obviously each Driver has his own tablet.) If they're still kept in a folder then Drivers will either photocopy them as required (yes, this is as wasteful as it sounds) or even jot down the details in their own notebook or a scrap piece of paper.

So…'SH02', 'M-F', '0335-1100' and '15/06-02/12'. 'SH02' would denote 'Shady Depot shift number 2' (if the shift was based at Shady Depot and was the second shift of the working day – that would mean there was a shift, SH01, which started even earlier than 0335…yuck). If it was Skankville Depot the abbreviation at the top of their schedules might be 'SK01' (I haven't spent long on these imaginary depot names, sue me.) 'M-F' means this particular shift runs from Monday to Friday. Therefore, on a Saturday, a similar shift to this would have the abbreviation 'SO' for 'Saturday Only' instead of 'M-F' on the schedule.

'0335-1100' is of course the actual time of day of the shift. Some companies will add the length of the shift in here as well (in our case it would have been 7hrs 25mins.) And finally, there are the dates through which this shift is expected to run, from June 15th to December 2nd. After this date, the company may issue new schedules which can be quite different from the previous ones. Often, if services have been performing well, the shift will simply reappear with new dates showing it running for another 6 months.

Other headings are 'Traction', 'Headcode', 'Action' for whatever action must be carried out, 'Dep' for 'Departs' and 'Arr' for 'Arrives'. 'Traction' is really just a fancy word for 'train' and refers to the particular type of train which will be used for that trip. Below these headings would be our particular information. For example, we could have a '101' train working the first part, a '103' train working the second, and another '101' train working the last journey. I've used random numbers as examples but in real life this would show something like '412' if it was an InterCity Express ('ICE') in Germany, or '390' if it was a Virgin 'Pendolino' in the UK. More information on traction or train identification can be found here : https://en.wikipedia.org/wiki/British_Rail_locomotive_and_multiple_unit_numbering_and_classification#1973_numbering_and_classification_-_TOPS . Although this pertains to the UK, other countries have similar systems.

The Headcode (or Train Reporting Number, or whatever other designation is given in different countries) identifies one single train. So the train you know as the 0730 from Sleepy Hollow, arriving at Upper Spinach at 0845, may be '1D12' to the Driver and other rail staff. Headcodes, at least in the UK, basically work as follows : the '1' is the 'Class' of train, the 'D' suggests its destination, and the '12' simply means it's the 12th train on that route since services began that day. Class 1 trains in the UK are 'express passenger trains' and are given priority over lower Classes, for example when they both try to approach a busy junction at the same time ('Class 2' is an 'ordinary passenger train' and the numbers continue with Freights coming into the picture at '3' and beyond, see here for a full explanation https://en.wikipedia.org/wiki/Train_reporting_number .)

Obviously the 'Dep' and 'Arr' are departure and arrival times for trains or taxis, or if you're a Freight Driver you may be required to drive a company car or van for part of your shift.

Now, to the 'Action'. This might show 'MOB' as the first action of your day. This denotes 'Mobilise' (different companies and countries use different terms) which basically means 'Get your train ready to move.' This varies among different types of train and whether they've been fully or partially shut down. Sometimes this can be as simple as inserting your key and allowing systems to self-test. Sometimes certain systems require you to press particular buttons to activate or acknowledge them.

Next, your train must depart the depot, say at '0355', and arrive at the station at '0415'. Then in the 'Action' column we might have 'REVERSE' – again this can vary, but it simply means closing down the cab you just used to drive into the station, walking to the cab at the other end of the train, and getting it ready for departure. Your headcode will alter if you're driving an empty train into the station to become a passenger service. So, something like '5P60', which denotes a 'Class 5' empty passenger train – would alter to '1P60' at the point you change ends in the station. You've miraculously transformed from an empty passenger train to an express passenger train.

Now the real work begins. You might be scheduled to work the 0445 departure from 'Shady Station', arriving at 'Bulbous Station' (wow, I really should find better names) at 0545. The train is continuing onward to its ultimate destination. How would we know? If it shows the next action as 'REL BY BS03 at 0546.' This means you are to be relieved at Bulbous Station at 0546 by the Driver working Bulbous Depot's BS03 shift. This Driver should be waiting for your arrival, probably where your cab door will stop on the platform. Then you might have an official 'BREAK' for just over an hour. Breaks are strictly controlled by regulations, ultimately from the government of the day, to ensure that Train Drivers are never so fatigued that the safety of trains is endangered. It's one thing to nod off in your car, quite another at the front of 8 coaches containing several hundred passengers at 100mph. As the old joke goes "When I die, I want to go like my father. Quietly, in his sleep. Not screaming and terrified, like his passengers."

After the break, you're likely to see something like 'REL BS05 AT 0659.' As you've already guessed, this means you are to relieve the Driver of Bulbous Depot shift BS05 at 0659. The next line tells you the Class of Traction (which may be different from the previous journey), the Headcode - say '1K49', and that you're due to depart at 0700. Let's say you arrive at Skankville Station at 0830 and 'IMMOB' – yes, this means 'Immobilise', which can be as simple as closing down the cab and taking your Driver's key out. You may have another short break at points like this, but this is not classed as an 'official' break – you just got lucky with timings. You might next relieve a Skankville Depot Driver at 0914 (say, shift SK07) on 101 Traction, and work 1L55 at 0915 to Shady Station, arriving at 1015. Your work is done!

The last part of the Schedule might show you travelling at 1030 in a taxi back to where you started and where your car awaits you, at Shady Depot, arriving at 1050. The shift would actually end at 1100 – the final 10 minutes are there to allow you to make your way from your taxi, put your equipment back in your locker, and check nothing requires your attention in the admin room (or indeed fill in any forms required). As you can imagine, the 'Action' column tends to have the most variety, with all kinds of abbreviations including 'WALK', 'SHUT DOWN' (the train, not your emotional sensibilities), 'PREP' (for 'Preparation' – that's when you may do an extensive walk round and multiple checks on that train) and many others.

Now back to our procedures at the start of a day...

2. Operational Information. This is up to date information on things you need to know for the particular routes and trains you will be working. For example, since you finished work the day before, engineers might have discovered a flaw in a bridge you will pass over. The speed over the bridge may have been 75mph yesterday, but if you did that today then you and your passengers, or freight cargo, could end up in the river. Today the speed may now be 20mph (maybe even 10mph for Freight, which tend to have heavier loads, so the pressure on the bridge from each axle on each wagon is greater than for Passenger services which weigh less.) As you can imagine, this stuff is pretty important – Drivers can get some nasty surprises if they don't take the time to read this material properly.

3. Updated Operational Publications. Depending as ever on company or country, these could be regular minor updates or periodical major updates to a variety of operating publications. More important publications may be handed over by Supervisors/Managers and require an immediate signature (legally certifying that you have received it, you will read it and you will understand it – if you then kill passengers or destroy a small town with your Freight train due to not following one of the new procedures, this ensures your company can blame you.)

4. At this point you might telephone or fax an application for any leave you require. If you telephone (and actually get a response at 0335 in the morning) then you might get an early indication of your chances of getting the day off. This ranges from "Yes, no problem." to "Hmm. Not looking good. There are 4 already in the system for that day." Rail companies often have a set number of staff who are guaranteed a day off based on the order in which they apply. So if your company guarantees only 2 Drivers off and there are 3 existing applicants, your chances are not good.

Sometimes people change their arrangements at the last moment and may cancel their application, bumping you up a place. Depending on annual budgets and staff goodwill, sometimes companies may even ask another Driver to work on his day off in order to allow you your leave day. The other Driver will be paid overtime for this so it's not as altruistic as it sounds. And sometimes you just have to change your plans as the company says "No." The guaranteed number of staff allowed leave each day is usually agreed between unions and management, and depends on the staff likely to be available to cover. Short version : it's often neither straightforward nor easy to get time off exactly when you need it, particularly at short notice.

5. Locker time. Now you find yourself in the locker room, if you have one. Sometimes lockers are just jammed in any available space, but they do tend to have working locks (although Supervisors have a master key, so it's not the place to store that contraband/superhero costume/severed head etc. – these should obviously be stored in your 'special basement.') IN THE OLD DAYS, Train Drivers were provided with quality leather bags or satchels, and older Drivers can still sometimes be seen with these. More recently, a wide variety of 'Driver luggage' has appeared, and some companies are tolerant of staff using their own.

Company-issue rucksacks are now seen, decorated with high-visibility strips and patches to aid visibility when Drivers are walking trackside, or in depots and yards. There have been many attempts to standardise Drivers' equipment within particular countries. While this may seem trivial, there is usually a safety aspect as well as a 'brand' or aesthetic consideration.

"Things That Can Happen While You're Driving A Train"

One of the tricky areas in railway operations involves Guards coming into the cab. There are rules governing this circumstance in most countries, some stricter than others. The Guard on a passenger train, particularly on a long-distance journey, may have reasons to talk to the Driver. This could be anything from a grumpy passenger who may be going to cause trouble later in the journey, to liaising with you regarding the late-running of the train and passengers trying to make connections at later stations.

Some Guards – and I always sympathised with their plight - would come up to their Driver's cab purely to put subtle pressure on the Driver, because they had a bunch of people who would miss a connection unless the train recovered a few minutes of late running. The only way to do this is to keep the train right on the maximum speed limit at all times, brake slightly later for stations (which could only be done in good weather and by skilled Drivers) and hope the Signallers will give you some help when you get to conflicting junctions. A lot of Drivers just didn't bother – why place your personal safety record in jeopardy in order to make up a few minutes of lost time? Others saw it as part of their professional responsibility, as long as it could be done safely. Let's be clear : officially you don't do it. Ever.

IN THE OLD DAYS some Drivers would recover late running by driving well over the speed limit on straighter sections of track, and slightly over the speed limit on curved sections. A lot of time could indeed be made up this way, but it was always at the risk of being caught speeding. Always a strange one that...Drivers speeding to ensure their company's customers are less late, are punished by their company for speeding. Of course, track speeds are there for a reason. Those are the speeds the engineers have deemed safe for those areas of track. If it was acceptable to go 5mph faster then the track speed would be 5mph higher. So, to sum up : speeding on trains rarely happens and is a serious disciplinary issue when it does (some Drivers speed through inattention or indeed confusion when they are new to a route). Most modern trains are fitted with data recorders and these are downloaded regularly. Any train found exceeding speed limits in an excessive or persistent fashion will result in its Driver being held to account.

Sometimes the Driver requires the Guard – if there is a tricky fault on the train it's sometimes possible for the Guard to help in getting more information or actually resetting a breaker which could clear the fault. Often, these things can be done over the internal communication system. But sometimes the Guard may not want the conversation to be overheard by passengers, or wants to have a face to face conversation if the situation is tricky or serious.

"What's the problem with the Guard coming to the cab?" I hear some of you say. Well, I was told some years ago of a Guard on a high-speed service who offered a Driver a cup of coffee from the onboard catering, towards the end of a long shift. All sounds very team-spirited and good-natured, yes? Which it was. Except that the Guard, by sheer bad luck, came into the cab with the cup of coffee at the very moment the Driver should have started braking for the next station (I should mention that, in the story I was told, the Driver had only recently begun driving these trains). By the time the Driver took the cup of coffee from the Guard, and placed it safely to one side, he realised he was now rapidly approaching his next station stop and began braking. It was too late. He couldn't stop in time. I never heard how this situation was subsequently tackled (there are strict rules in that country regarding trains not stopping in time at a station) but both employees were apparently hauled up in front of their respective managers.

It's a tricky area. You certainly don't want incidents like the one above, or others with worse consequences, but you also don't want to lose the human interaction between staff. It not only helps in terms of teamwork, it reduces the loneliness of the Driver's job.

Back to the locker room at your depot, and you might now transfer your food and beverages into your Driver's satchel. Or you may go with a company-issue satchel/personal rucksack combo (small laptops and tablets are becoming popular – just don't plug one in on company property below one of the subtle signs which state 'NO PERSONAL ELECTRONIC EQUIPMENT IS TO BE CONNECTED TO THE MAINS WITHOUT PERMISSION'.) Aside from whatever personal belongings you're carrying, all rail companies have a list of 'essential' items or 'minimum' equipment which must be carried by a Driver. Most will include the following (all company-issue) :

* Driver's keys
* Driver's manuals
* High-visibility clothing
* Travel pass
* Sunglasses
* Tablet or laptop
* Torch or Lamp
* Mobile phone
* Official forms

Let's take a look at those in detail.

Driver's Minimum Equipment

Driver's Keys

Depending on the country we're talking about and the type of trains you drive, much of the time you will require a specialised key to unlock the control desk in the driving cab. In these stabby/shooty/bomby times, most trains have locked cab doors requiring another specialised key. Also, depending on locations you visit, you may require further keys to unlock gates, trackside cabins or equipment. In the UK, rail staff often carry a 'carriage key', which can open all kinds of cupboards and panels both onboard trains and elsewhere – apparently a remnant of the former national rail company, 'British Rail', before it was privatised.

Driver's Manuals

I'm told companies in the UK now tend to produce a general manual, called a 'General Appendix' or 'General Instructions' or similar. This covers general operational procedures on a day to day basis plus detailed instructions on subjects such as defective equipment, extreme weather, unusual situations like suicides, and most other things you can imagine. Often this general manual is written in a way that it can be used by all operations staff, not just Drivers. The better ones will highlight how the duties of different staff members complement one another to produce an effective team performance in dealing with operational situations.

In addition to a general manual, Drivers have individual manuals for each different type of train they drive. These describe in varying levels of detail how each unit/locomotive/train works, followed by usually large sections covering every conceivable defect which might occur – circuit breaker tripping and brakes applying, lights go out in first and last carriage only, door comes open on a freight vehicle, cow lands on cab roof (wait, that must have been another dream.) There will follow detailed instructions on how to remedy each of these defects. Or not fix them should they prove unfixable ("The cow refuses to come down. Says he's not moooooving.") IN THE OLD DAYS many Drivers tried, and were often expected, to memorise many of these defects and their remedies. Thanks to Health and Safety legislation, lawyers, and vast insurance bills, many companies now require their Drivers to call a 'maintenance' number for expert help. Similar to what airline companies have been doing for many years.

Some companies produce manuals on how to actually drive the trains. This sounds fairly sensible but they are often frowned upon by older Drivers. Traditions die hard, and in the days of steam trains, the way to learn was by 'doing', and not 'reading manuals'. Outsiders will see merit in both viewpoints.

Freight Drivers may have additional manuals concerning types of hazardous freight, freight vehicles, and other freight-specific technical issues. Yes, unsurprisingly, driving a train carrying explosives is different from driving a train full of passengers. Except on Saturday nights, of course.

High Visibility Clothing

This could be a vest or a coat, or both. They can be yellow, green, or orange, depending on location and company. Drivers are generally required to wear HVC whenever they go trackside. This allows other Drivers in oncoming trains to see them from a greater distance (or at all, in darkness or poor visibility) and blow the train horn to warn them they are approaching. Incredible as it may sound, Drivers are still killed in the 21st century while trackside, whether attending to a train defect or engrossed in some other duty. Near misses – where the oncoming train narrowly avoids striking someone – continue to occur.

It's worth mentioning that the modern high-visibility safety vest is an excellent example of an evolved design. Older versions included sturdy buttons with buttonholes, built to last. These were changed to Velcro or pop-studs, after various incidents involving the vests and their wearers becoming snagged by passing vehicles…

Travel Pass

A shift may involve travel on another company's trains. For example, you might drive a train to a distant location but would wait a long time to return on one of your own company's trains (assuming you can't drive a train back, perhaps for regulations to do with Breaks.) Clearly this is not productive. So travelling back on another company's train, even at some cost, may prove more efficient. Because this is indeed required among so many companies and staff, a reduced cost system may be created (as in the UK), where Drivers are provided with a 'Travel Pass' which allows them to travel on other companies' trains. These are emblazoned with phrases like 'FOR DUTY PURPOSES ONLY' and 'NOT FOR LEISURE TRAVEL'. So, before you ask, no. It can't be used for a day at the beach. Actually you could, if you were crazy enough to wear your company uniform to the beach. But all it would require is for the Ticket Examiner or Guard to ask to see your work schedule…and then your whole career could be in jeopardy.

Sunglasses

Surely you would want the Driver at the front of your 100mph train to, you know, see properly? Sunglasses are simply essential when the sun is low in the sky. Funnily enough, problems can arise due to different tinted lenses affecting colour perception. "Was that a Green or Red signal? Ah, probably Green…Oh no! Aaaaaarrrgghhh!" And he's attacked by killer bees. No, it's those dreams again…But you see the problem. Companies now issue sunglasses which avoid all these issues.

Tablet or Laptop

If it's not a tablet it's usually a smaller laptop or notebook. This has been a growing trend in the industry for some time. Heavy, environmentally dubious and user-unfriendly manuals are being replaced by portable electronic devices. These are much easier to update (automatically, instead of manually removing pages/throwing old ones in the bin/inserting new ones) and dramatically reduce the weight of the Driver's bag/rucksack so that Drivers don't end up like crumpled, groaning characters from a Dickens' book. Companies are also keen to use them for general staff communication.

Mobile Phone

Because things can change so dramatically from one moment to the next on the railway (1428 on a Sunny afternoon : everything's fine, 1430: tall truck hits a rail bridge, the line's closed for at least an hour etc.), it became obvious that providing Drivers with mobile phones was a good idea. These may be for company business only (that expensive international call WILL be noticed by someone somewhere in the company, and you WILL be billed) and there are rigorous instructions regarding their use. Following a multiple fatality crash in California in 2008 (see 'Chatsworth' below), strict rules were enacted internationally to ensure Train Drivers would not be distracted by mobile phones while driving. Some Drivers actually prefer to keep company mobiles switched off as much as possible, as it stops the company from phoning up and asking for favours, like working on your day off. It's worth stating, however, that railways run on favours.

Chatsworth

On Friday, September 12th, 2008, a Passenger train collided with a Freight train in the Chatsworth area of Los Angeles. 25 people were killed, including the Driver of the Passenger

train. You can find the full report here :
https://www.ntsb.gov/investigations/AccidentReports/Pages/RAR1001.aspx Investigators found that the Driver of the Passenger train had been sending text messages to 'railway enthusiasts' at multiple times during his shift, with the final one being sent just seconds before the collision. The National Transportation and Safety Board concluded that he had been so distracted by his mobile phone that he had passed a red signal – allowing his train to enter a single line track without authority and colliding head-on with the Freight train. By sheer bad luck (which frequently plays a part in both rail and aviation incidents), the timing of the incident saw the trains meet on a sharp curve, and in addition the Freight had just emerged from a tunnel, reducing the time for both Drivers to see and react to each other's trains.

Although there were rules of varying severity already in existence in several countries, the Chatsworth incident quite correctly saw a severe tightening up of these regulations. Mobile phone use while driving trains is today effectively banned in several countries, though this is no consolation to those families who lost loved ones at Chatsworth. In the UK, these restrictions are enforced rigorously, and Drivers with personal mobile phones in addition to their company ones must be careful to ensure they are switched off before driving begins.

Torch or Lamp

Much as a new Driver might like to think 'I'll never need this', you most definitely will. At some point, perhaps at 0200 on a moonless night next to a failed Freight train in the middle of a forest, or underneath some supposedly ultra-modern Passenger train while searching for an obscure handle/switch which requires pulling/switching, you will be grateful for the humble torch. Variants often include red, green and yellow settings for handsignalling to trains/other staff.

Driver's Forms

Once again, these vary among companies and countries, but comprise a series of forms which MUST be filled out in certain circumstances. For example, you might have particular forms for Signalling faults. If you come across a Signal that is changing colour continually (even if you're on a different track and see this) you will be required to report it at the time by radio or telephone (at a Signal, or Station, or using cab equipment) and also fill out a specialised Signalling fault form, which will act as a record for your own and other companies.

So that's the minimum equipment to be carried at all times. Drivers usually like to carry additional items like gloves (essential for Freight Drivers, who mainly deal with oily/dusty locomotives, although Passenger Drivers can find themselves reaching into oily/dusty/dead-wildlife encrusted areas), wipes or paper towels, spare keys (it's really not ideal to have 7 minutes to departure and realise you've misplaced the Driver's key which unlocks the controls), and other items which vary with the company and the individual. You may have chuckled when watching a lady friend emptying her handbag, but I've watched Drivers emptying their official Driver's bag and wondered if there was some kind of magic at work – where the hell is it all coming from?

Now you've got all your gear, it's finally time to drive a train! Or perhaps 'Prepare' one – we'll get to that shortly. You leave the Drivers area and head for wherever the trains/locomotives are stabled. All larger depots have a building or buildings where maintenance is carried out. This may be called a 'shed' (particularly in the UK) but can vary substantially in size from a small building, just large enough to house one locomotive/vehicle, to a large, movie-studio scale beast which can accommodate ten or more full-length Passenger trains. Many trains or locos are left outside overnight, having already been worked on by maintenance staff, or not requiring any attention. In bad weather, in the middle of the night, you will be hoping that your train is indoors somewhere (particularly if you're going to spend 30 minutes or more 'preparing' it). If it's nice and sunny you'll want it outside. Of course, 50% of the time it'll most definitely be the opposite of what you're hoping for.

"Railway Matters"

In the early 21st century, the rail industry began making a serious attempt to follow the aviation industry in having most trains carry data recorders, or 'black boxes'. New trains would have them as standard, and older trains would be subject to retrofitting. In safety terms, these have been an enormous positive in the industry, allowing precise determination of a Train Driver's actions during incidents. From a Driver's viewpoint, they have been a mixed bag. As many Drivers will say, "If you're doing your job properly you have nothing to fear". Others bemoaned the fact that every minor error, which in the past would have caused the Driver on the day a bit of a fright and hopefully been an excellent learning point, were now being jumped on by managers.

Some Drivers were even caught out by their misbehaving colleagues – when an incident occurred and the recorder was downloaded, checks were made on the train's entire day in service, sometimes resulting in a Driver's error from earlier in the day coming to light. The data recorder is sometimes referred to in the UK as 'the spy in the cab'. Personally, it didn't bother me, although it came in towards the end of my career. As a Driver, you're aware that your mistakes are likely to end up in some form of investigation. So having a recorder present, as far as I was concerned, simply meant the evidence was going to be that bit more precise.

Back to our working day, and the walk to the shed may be quite long, depending on the size of your depot. As you can imagine, country depots are easily traversed in a few minutes, while some city depots could do with their own internal transport – still, it'll help to keep you fit, and that's a good thing considering how much of your working life will be spent sitting on your backside. You may well encounter more animal 'friends', or even other exhausted colleagues nearing the middle or end of a long nightshift. More witty banter may ensue…

You : "Hey."

Colleague :   "What you working?"

You : "4.45."

Colleague :   "Yuck."

And away he walks. Or, if it's one of your friendlier colleagues, he may stop for a chat. All Drivers will report to colleagues anything they might need to know ("There was a major emergency repair required tonight, so they're running late on everything.") Usually at larger depots there are also a variety of staff around, depending on the time of day – maintenance, cleaners, and others. You will have to find out exactly where the train intended for your service is, and this requires either a visit to a Supervisor's office or a call to a nominated person. Finally, you find yourself approaching your train

4

Preparing The Train/Getting Onboard

There are still some companies, at the time of writing, who have Drivers 'prepare' or 'prep' the train. Most companies are moving away from this, as a Maintenance Technician – whose technical knowledge of the train is much more detailed than any Driver's – should already have given the train a thorough inspection. This is another relic from bygone days when Drivers were required to have far greater technical knowledge of the trains. Older Drivers, in particular, have not been keen to reduce the Driver's role by abolishing 'Prep'. Not only will less knowledge be required by future Drivers, but a certain confidence in the safety and readiness of the train will also be lost. Should you work for one of the remaining 'prep' companies, you will now be required to follow a precise list of checks, both inside and outside of the train.

First, you will deposit your Driver's bag in the cab you intend to drive from. Then you can begin the list of specific checks, as specified in each company's Driver's manual (or manual for that particular type of train). If you're lucky the company may provide you with laminated cards or sheets with the checks listed on them. These often fit easier in a coat pocket and are particularly helpful to new Drivers. After a few weeks, as long as you're doing it regularly, you'll be able to do it by memory.

"Things That Can Happen While You're Driving A Train"

I've heard a few phrases on the list of 'Sentences That Must Have Rarely Been Uttered On Planet Earth' when it comes to cows on the line. One Driver, reporting the lengthy saga of his incident after hitting a cow at high speed (the train, not the cow – you guys are all comedians), was asked by the Signaller "What is the status of the cow?" The Driver, who probably found the Signaller's overzealous attempt to sound professional amusing at some later date, did not sound happy at receiving such a question, given that he had been driving at over 100mph at the time of the impact. His terse reply was pretty much spat into the radio microphone, "I killed it".

Another Driver was cautioned for cows on the track, and finding they were in a quite different place from the reported location (which is dangerous, because hitting a cow at speed can have serious consequences - see the Polmont accident in the UK https://en.wikipedia.org/wiki/Polmont_rail_accident), decided to call the Signaller back on the radio. Without thinking, he began his radio message with "I just wanted to give you a cow update." Apparently it was obvious to listeners at the time that the Signaller and Driver had problems keeping their voices 'professional', as both sensed the ridiculous nature of the terminology.

In truth, hitting an animal as large as a cow is no laughing matter. Although various design modifications mean it is extremely unlikely that a train could be derailed, the impact can be quite dramatic. And, if you really want to know, the blood, organic matter and smell aren't much fun either. Drivers are required to inspect their trains immediately after this type of impact...

'Preps' consist of variations on the following tasks, with two main areas :

1. **Walking around the exterior of the train**. You will look for obvious defects/damage, any doors/handles/switches/latches/pipes/cupboard or panel doors not being in their correct position, correct indications on exterior gauges, and if applicable, correct sand in sandboxes (yes, we still blast sand from a pipe directed at the wheels and operated by a button in the cab, when things get very slippy).

When maintenance staff are actively working on a train, they place some form of warning board ('NOT TO BE MOVED' etc.) on the train itself. This should stop any hasty Drivers or other staff trying to start or move the train or loco while staff are working. Occasionally these boards – which should be removed at the conclusion of maintenance work – are forgotten about, and this is another item Drivers will be checking.

2. **Walking through the interior of the train**. Stepping over unconscious, drunken passengers who forgot to get off (joking of course, such things never happen…no, no…absolutely no passengers have ever ended up in a maintenance depot late at night and been shepherded discreetly into a taxi back to the

station...no siree). The main tasks usually involve checking safety equipment – fire extinguishers, light sticks, window hammers and anything else your company or country has deemed worth installing for public use. Most passenger vehicles now also have their own particular cupboards and panels where all kinds of circuit breakers, gauges, switches and handles may require checking. Onboard shops on Passenger trains are sometimes stocked and often locked, to be unlocked and readied by other staff at the departure station.

On locomotives (mostly used for Freight in places like the UK) the interior walk is a cramped and oily adventure. Essential gauges, circuit breakers, handles, switches, and various other equipment must be inspected, as well as the usual lookout for any obvious defects or damage. This may all have to be performed while adopting a variety of bodily positions due to the cramped interior, and manipulating a torch in order to see everything properly.

At either end of the interior walk is the Driver's main focus : cab checks. Cab checks can be quite thorough (for obvious reasons) and the Driver who is foolish enough to skip any or all of them will eventually be found out, possibly in an embarrassing manner (for example, if the train breaks down a few hundred metres out of the depot due to a fault which could have been easily found and remedied).

At some point during the Prep the train will have to actually be started up. This can range from a fairly straightforward procedure on modern electric trains –

involving pressing a few buttons in a certain sequence – to a trickier, noisier and more involved ritual on older diesel locomotives. Part of the start up procedure is ensuring all systems are operating at their correct pressures/temperatures etc. If an older model of locomotive takes a while to get all its systems up and running, then the Prep is written so that the Driver carries out other checks in the meantime, and isn't standing around waiting.

Standard cab checks include : checking or testing the braking system/lights/wipers/windscreen wash/on-train and external communication/speedometer /driving controls/bell or buzzer communication/isolation switches and levers/circuit breakers/cab and train heating or cooling/door control equipment, and various safety systems.

One of the relatively well-known safety systems in the UK is the 'Driver's Safety Device' or 'Dead Man's Pedal'. This is exactly what it sounds like. A pedal at the Driver's feet which is intended to halt the train should the Driver, for whatever reason, become unconscious/dead/deceased/pop his clogs/shuffle off the mortal coil etc. In normal train driving, the Driver will sit with his foot or feet holding this pedal down. Should the pedal be released when the train is moving (some systems tie it into the 'Forward/Reverse' control on the desk) then after a short interval, anywhere around the 5 seconds mark, all the brakes on the train will be fully applied. Of course, should the Driver have a heart attack and fall forward with his weight still on the pedal, you're in trouble (you're really not – the 'Vigilance' system, which sounds loud beeps every 30 or 60 seconds in order to keep the Driver awake, will put the brakes on if the DSD pedal is not raised and lowered pretty sharpish at the beeps).

In case you think railways are getting all 'high-tech', another check that is done is on cab emergency equipment. This tends to consist of things like red flags (that's right – all that might be between you and your just-derailed train being slammed by an oncoming express train is a member of staff frantically waving a red flag in the air), specialised sets of clips to operate signalling in an emergency, and detonators. You heard right. This is a small set of explosive devices which are intended for placing on the actual rails, and again are intended for stopping trains in an emergency situation. Drivers who are lucky enough to have company simulators may be tested by having their train running over detonators unexpectedly. As you can imagine, the official instructions in these situations is to stop your train immediately…

"Things That Can Happen While You're Driving A Train"

A big part of Driver training is to prepare you for emergency situations, and to train you to 'fault-find' on trains. While these sound quite different on the face of it, they actually share a lot of similarities. Both require you to amass information as quickly and methodically as possible, then to apply particular training as precisely as possible in order to resolve the situation. I never had any fires but I did have the fire system go off in error several times. That's an experience that gets the adrenaline flowing – bells ringing, desk indications flashing. In terms of faults, I had quite a few and they were all different. If you're a good professional then you keep all the relevant information close at hand – whether this is carrying manuals or having the company tablet or even your own smartphone with the relevant files loaded. And, of course, remembering your training.

There are almost as many faults on different trains as there are stars in the sky. This is an exaggeration, but you get the point. And after years of working on a particular class of train and getting to know all its faults and quirks, your company introduces a shiny new train straight out of the factory. There will follow at least six months where everyone – even the guy in the Maintenance office on the end of the emergency breakdown number – is trying to learn the never-before-seen faults and how to fix them.

There has increasingly been a move towards Drivers becoming less proactive in fault-finding, with a preference for them to phone a number where someone in an office (often an employee of the train manufacturer) consults manuals or computer software and relates the actions to take. Many Drivers see this as another 'de-skilling', while some are glad to have all the responsibility and pressure of the fault-finding situation somewhat removed from the Driver's shoulders. Some companies have fault-finding information on the company tablet. This is an area where the industry is still experimenting to find the best solution.

A check which all good Drivers make, whether it's required or not, is to have a look at several of the most recent repairs which have been done to that particular train. Most companies have a 'Repair Book' or 'Maintenance Log' or similar – this is simply a book, kept in the cab of the train, which is used to record defects and (hopefully) subsequent repairs. If you check it and find an entry from the day before, and no-one has written anything with regard to 'Action Taken', you'd be phoning pretty quickly to see whether that work was done or not. Similar books are seen in the cockpits of aircraft, and in a similar fashion, these books can be a window into the levels of respect or otherwise between frontline staff and maintenance staff. A famous Repair Book exchange, quoted both in the UK rail and airline industries (though where it actually occurred, if it really did, is unclear) read as follows :

DEFECT : Something rattling in cab.

ACTION TAKEN : Something repaired in cab.

The airline version has 'cockpit' instead of 'cab' but is identical. Some of these exchanges became quite heated, and this display of adult professionalism continues to this day…Can't lie – it is funny. Companies had always had a box in these books where the staff member reporting the defect was supposed to write their name, and the maintenance person filling in the 'ACTION TAKEN' section was supposed to supply theirs too. However, many staff simply wrote an unintelligible scrawl so that they couldn't be traced and admonished for their sarcasm.

The final set of checks will be done in the cab which you intend to use to leave the depot. If all is well after these, then you simply wait for a designated member of the depot staff to appear just before your departure time and signal you to depart. This varies from depot to depot, with older depots still having a member of staff wave the train away with handsignals. Modern depots tend to have colour light signals, although this still requires a member of depot staff to operate them. Once you receive your signal, you can get your train moving to the depot exit.

5

Depot to Station

You're actually driving a train!

Although, in a depot, you're probably moving at around 3-5mph and looking out carefully for staff on the ground. Depots have 'train washes' – these are pretty much identical to your automatic car wash, except there's often no brush to clean the roof due to roof equipment associated with overhead electrical cables, those ones that supply power to your train…Most depots try to have their train wash in a position where trains can pass through it easily (hopefully during the night when cleaning and maintenance are done) and not slow things up during the day. Depots also have teams of cleaning and maintenance staff, so they can be very busy places – particularly at night – and considerable caution must be exercised when moving about in a train.

Anyway, you're finally moving. If you're unlucky you might hear a buzzing or a beeping or a ringing, perhaps with a flashing light on the desk in front of you. This doesn't happen often, but it's not a good start to your driving day if it does. It means there's a fault of some kind on the train, and one which only registers when the train starts to move. You have no choice but to stop and inform the maintenance team (who may be within a hundred yards of you, anyway), although if you stop while leaving a depot there tend to be a bunch of people wanting to know what you're playing at pretty quickly. It's very frustrating, particularly given the fact that maintenance staff may have already spent hours working on your train (which, of course, can actually cause such problems). At least help is close at hand.

"Things That Can Happen While You're Driving A Train"

You can't have trains without track to run them on. Or signals to keep the trains apart. There's a whole army of jobs dedicated to maintaining track or signals. These men or women are to be seen out in all weather, at all times of the day and night, working away to keep the trains running. Occasionally one of them will appear at a station and come for a run in your cab (with a cab pass of course, and for official purposes). This is as close as Drivers will get to what are loosely termed 'trackworkers', although there may be different terms in your own country. Most of the time we see them from up in our cab, often in bad weather, and think 'Well, anytime I get annoyed at my job, I remember there are plenty people on the railway doing proper manual labour'.

The other thing to say about trackworkers is that they can give you some major scares. This can occur when one or more of them has taken some kind of chance with the various protection systems which are supposed to warn them of approaching trains. The worst part of this is that these are often dedicated people who are actually trying to complete their work, and are pressured into taking a chance at some point in order to complete an unrealistic work schedule. Don't get me wrong – this is not the norm, but it does happen and many Drivers have stories about a scare due to trackworkers. By the regulations, these sort of incidents should always be reported, but many Drivers will admit that they didn't report it because they thought they would be getting someone into trouble. Of course, if such a scare really did constitute what is known as a 'near miss' then it absolutely would be reported. Thankfully, today's railway is a lot more safety-oriented, and stories of this type are becoming rarer with each passing year.

At the depot exit stands the signal which leads to the outside world. You may have to call up the Signaller from here and let him know you're ready to depart. Sometimes there are procedures where the Signaller will automatically be aware of your approach to the exit. Hopefully the Signal will change fairly quickly so that you can depart on time.

The short trip from depot to station is an opportunity to get a feel for how your train is running, and shake off any of your own rustiness. If you've been on vacation then starting your return to work with a brief run on an empty train is preferable to going straight into some high-speed Passenger work or heavy Freight train situation. However, it's all down to dumb luck.

Once you pull clear of the depot you can get up some speed, and most countries require mandatory testing of the brakes at this point. To some readers this may seem a bit like overkill, but multiple incidents have happened after brake testing procedures weren't followed. Having little or no brakes on a moving train is not fun, and tends to end badly. Brake tests are worth a closer look.

Brake Tests

The 'running brake test' or whatever it's called in your country, is simply a way to check that your train will slow down in the expected manner, after you have got it up to speed for the first time. This may seem a little unnecessary, particularly just after leaving a depot, but there have been many accidents and less serious incidents involving poor, or non-functioning brakes, throughout railway history. In fact, leaving a depot might actually be one of the more likely times for such a scenario, as brakes or brake-associated systems may have been the subject of overnight repairs.

The other main brake test is when a locomotive is coupled to passenger vehicles or freight wagons. This is known as a 'brake continuity test', and as the name suggests it aims to prove that there is a continuous air supply for braking throughout the entire length of a train. After a member of staff has coupled the coupling onto the drawhook and then connected all the required pipes and cables, they will operate handles on the air pipes which will allow air to enter the first vehicle of the train. Assuming the train itself has been properly coupled together, there should now be air flowing to the rear end of the train.

Usually the same staff member will now walk to the back of the train and handsignal to the Driver that they are ready to perform a brake test. The Driver traps a certain pressure of air in the train's system with a particular movement of the main brake control in the cab (note that there are more modern variations on this now rather old test). He then handsignals back to the staff member at the back of the train, who will pull one of the handles on the pipes there. Air will vent from this pipe until all the 'trapped' air in the train escapes. If you've been in a railway station and heard this extremely loud blast of air which fades away within a few seconds, then you've been listening to a 'brake continuity test'. As the air vents from the back of the train the Driver observes his brake pressure gauge in the front cab, as it drops to zero. He then either gives a quick blast on the horn or simply operates the brake control again – the 'toot' of the horn or the sound of air at the back of the train is a signal for the staff member there that the test was a success, and the handle on the brake pipe can now be closed.

Again, you might feel that this test isn't strictly necessary as all the different components of this situation should already have been separately tested.

And again, I would draw your attention to railway history, which right up to recent times has a variety of incidents attributable to a continuity test either not being done or not being done properly. Anyone wishing to look at UK rail accident history could start with the well-known book 'Red For Danger' by LTC Rolt, or any concerning rail safety by Stanley Hall. There are also more recent books by other authors.

Once clear of the depot, you'll follow a series of signals, eventually arriving into the station platform which is scheduled for your departure. One of the things that can catch a Driver out at this point is the platform he's heading into. Particularly in the UK, trains can be longer than the platforms. This causes problems with arriving trains, should the last door be opened and someone tries to step out…There are all kinds of instructions and procedures which mean that a train shouldn't be ending up at a platform that is too short for it. But it still happens. There are all kinds of good and understandable reasons why it happens, but whatever the situation, it is the Driver's responsibility to ensure his train isn't in the wrong place.

I had several instances of Signallers trying to put my train into a platform that was too short for it. These sometimes occur when a train company has replaced the usual train with a longer one, and either not informed the Signaller or the message simply hasn't got all the way through to him. There are a number of ways of dealing with these situations, but in order to deal with them you first have to recognise them. There are Drivers who, for whatever reason, aren't concentrating as they should be at a particular moment, and don't realise they're taking their train into a platform which is too short for it. It's rare for passengers to actually open doors and fall out, but it's enough of a shock to the travelling public to open a train door and see a five-foot drop to the ground rather than a platform. And rail companies take these incidents very seriously, as you would expect. As with many aspects of Train Driving, concentration is key.

"Things That Can Happen While You're Driving A Train"

Let's be clear : if you're a Train Driver you're going to hit stuff. No, not obnoxious colleagues. Things on the track. And probably at some speed. Hopefully it won't be a human being or a road vehicle, but there's a high probability that you're going to be smashing into a branch/tree, earth/stones from a landslip, or some trackside engineering equipment or trackside materials not properly secured. Also, some unfortunate list of animals will become your victims. You never get used to it - neither the killing of animals or the massive shock when you plough into some obstruction.

It's both better and worse if you get some kind of warning by actually seeing what you're going to hit before it happens. Although seeing something that you have no real chance of stopping for, can actually increase the stress substantially. At least you're aware an impact is imminent. Whereas, it's not fun to have some large-sized bird take off from the lineside as you approach – without any possibility of you seeing it at all – and it slamming into the lower front of your train. You know you've hit 'something' but you had no chance to see what it was. This is definitely one for the 'Con' rather than 'Pro' column. And did I mention Drivers can't have weak hearts? You begin to see why.

Back to our working day, and thankfully most of the time your journey from the depot to the station platform will be uneventful. You've now cleared the cobwebs from your brain and your train, and soon the real work will begin.

6
At The Station

At the station you will finally be joined by colleagues. Depending on the company, these may include a Guard/Conductor/Ticket Examiner and an array of onboard catering staff. In Freight working you're basically on your own – although in the US and some countries the nature of the enormous trains means extra staff will be required. In UK Freight, you'll deal with a member of the staff at the Freight Yard immediately before departure. They will provide paperwork regarding today's train (it helps to know today's train is 1200 tonnes when yesterday's was only 800 – they behave differently, particularly when you're trying to stop the big beasts). On Freight, you would see that your loco is coupled correctly to the wagons, and then a 'brake continuity test' is done before departure.

"Only On The Railway?"

As a Driver, it was easy to forget what a rarefied place the cab of a train or locomotive can be to a member of the public. Sometimes at stations I would see a mother or father with their child, who were clearly only there because the child was a train fanatic. Like many Drivers, I would try to find the time to invite them into the cab. I can honestly say one of the biggest kicks I ever got from the job was seeing a kid sitting in the Driver's seat, often with his parent taking a picture as a memento. It was always very frustrating when I couldn't do this, either because there was some technical issue with the train and I was awaiting staff to assist, or I simply didn't have enough time. Late taxis, or actually being held up with the train coming in from the depot, were often the cause of a very tight window to get the front cab ready for departure. It was difficult to see some train fanatic and parent hovering around, and not be able to invite them in.

Some Drivers never do this, and I understand their stance. All it would take is for someone to slip and fall, either getting on or off the train, and you would be in a whole lot of trouble. I certainly did more of the 'cab photo op' near the end of my career, so perhaps I subconsciously judged the risk more worthwhile than a younger Driver with more to lose. I still wish I'd done more of it.

Back to the station, and if you were working a locomotive plus coaches then a 'brake continuity test' will be required after coupling. Drivers of 'multiple unit' trains (where engines and/or traction motors are suspended beneath coaches) don't have this issue – you brought the whole train with you! It's worth pointing out that, for example, in the UK Class 390 'Pendolino' tilting trains are classed as multiple units. So 'multiple unit' covers a wide spectrum of train – from small, 2-coach units which usually work lower-speed, shorter journeys on local services to high-speed, long-distance, 11-coach monsters. Multiple unit trains are 'fixed formation', so they comprise a base train as mentioned above. A 'standard Class 156' unit is 2 coaches, while a 'standard Class 390' is 11 coaches. Flexibility is possible through simply coupling up 2, 3 or even 4 units (which may themselves be 2,3, 4 or 5-coaches) to make a total train comprising anything from 4 to 16-coaches or more. Of course, there are regulations about the maximum number of combinations allowed, governed by platform lengths and a variety of technical issues.

If you do have to do a brake continuity test with your locomotive and coaches, then hopefully a designated member of station staff is already waiting for you when you arrive. As we know, the brake continuity test basically proves that the brake system has an air supply from your locomotive to the very rear of the train. To recap, the station staff member proves this by simply venting the air pipe at the back – if the pipe didn't have continuity then air wouldn't come rushing out. Multiple units tend to bring electronics into the question of 'continuity' these days, but the basic principle that there is a working braking system throughout the length of the train still applies.

"Railway Matters"

One of the trickiest things a Freight Driver may be involved in is engineering work. This would be the situation when he's the Driver of the train which brings either engineering equipment or materials into the area where the work is to take place. There are substantial and detailed rules governing these situations. However, given the complexity of these engineering operations, with large amounts of machinery and staff working against demanding time pressures, the scope for mishaps is large.

Add in complicating factors such as frequent work during the night, bad weather, and technical issues with equipment delaying work, and you begin to see why it's remarkable that so much is actually achieved. With the pressure the engineering staff are under (including the managers), it's no wonder that there are sometimes unofficial requests to Drivers to bend their rules a little. Good Drivers don't bend the rules. But, certainly in the past, this is one of the times you would be asked – usually in a roundabout way – to do so.

Today, the rules continue to tighten and any irregularities are the subject of fairly comprehensive investigation. The use of outside companies has added to the complexities of engineering operations, particularly in the UK, but successive official 'reviews' have tended to urge closer collaboration between companies. Balancing efficiency and safety has been a key challenge in railways around the world, and being the

Driver of an engineering train will certainly give you a vivid and very practical experience of that.

Back to our working day, and at a terminal station the front of your empty train from the depot is now the rear of your outward passenger service. This means you'll be walking to the other end of the train and opening up that cab. Had you arrived at the station in a taxi – as opposed to bringing the train in empty yourself – the first thing you would do is enter the rear cab, find the Maintenance Repair Book, and see if the previous Driver reported any faults you need to know about.

At some point, you may or may not get a chance to exchange some pleasantries with the catering staff (like you, they have things to do before departure) but you will definitely have a conversation with your Guard (or whatever he/she is called in each company). They will provide any necessary paperwork – at a minimum this will be a list of the stations you must stop at. You will also discuss anything else noteworthy, such as disruption on the line ahead, weather warnings, VIP passengers or anything else that might affect you later in the journey.

Drivers always like to know if one of their managers is travelling on the train. It's not that Drivers will be slovenly reprobates unsupervised, but we will ensure we follow procedures rigidly if we know there is a manager around (of course, most modern trains have a

Data Recorder, so Drivers feel their managers are 'watching' them pretty much the whole time anyway).

Once you've had this essential conversation with your Guard, the last person you may see before departure is a member of maintenance staff. Some companies can afford the luxury of having 'roving' maintenance staff. They may travel on certain trains or hang around the busier stations, awaiting a call about a defect. If your company doesn't have them, and most don't, the only other people you will see are those travelling with you in the cab (if any). Let's have a quick look at that.

Cab Occupants

You won't be surprised to learn that there are very strict rules on anyone other than a Driver being in the cab. This is common sense – each additional person increases the potential for the Driver to be distracted at a critical moment. The most frequent cab visitors on trains are usually either Drivers from your own or other companies, or track maintenance staff. Drivers require access to cabs of other trains in order to either Route Learn or Route Refresh. Maintenance staff could be doing any number of inspections – from checking levels of flood water to checking how comfortable a ride the track is providing. If it's a route with overhead electric wires then they may be inspecting those.

The permissible cab visitors are laid down in the regulations. All visitors must be in possession of written authority to be in the cab. This often takes the form of a credit-card sized 'pass' with details on it regarding its valid dates, routes, and other pertinent data.

Guidance is also provided in the regulations with regard to 'cab visitor etiquette', such as not speaking to the Driver when he is approaching a station or red signal. Occasionally, and again in accordance with regulations, companies may allow members of the public to be in the cab in special circumstances. They are usually accompanied by rail management. Having said that, don't think you can just write to your local rail company and get yourself a run in a cab. These things happen rarely, and only in special circumstances. Your best chance of being a 'cab occupant' is still to get a Driver's job...

Once any cab occupants are dealt with, you are into your pre-departure routine. For many Drivers this simply means going to the toilet. For others, it may involve some final checks, such as ensuring the lighting on the front of the train is working (little panels in the cab should display which lights are currently lit – but many Drivers still like a look themselves). Whatever the deal, with around 5 minutes to departure time, most Drivers like to be sat in the seat and waiting to go.

Depending on how busy a station you're leaving, the red signal in front of you will change to a yellow or green, anytime from two minutes to ten seconds before you're due to leave. Strictly speaking, there are minimum times required to carry out the full departure process – for longer trains with more doors, and for older 'slammable' doors, this can take a lot longer. IN THE OLD DAYS Drivers were expected to hang out of the driving cab window and observe the despatch process, even responding to acknowledge the final handsignal from staff on the platform. Newer trains mean Drivers can often sit in the cab and await a small signal – situated below the main signal – which will tell him everything's okay and it's time to go. In the UK, this is achieved by lighting the letters 'RA' (for 'Right Away' – hey, it's tradition, man) just below the main signal.

This is your cue, Mr or Mrs Driver.

At last, you pull out the DRA switch (see 'Cab Controls' below), select 'Forward' on the Direction Selector, release the brakes, and move whatever controller you have on this machine into a power setting. At this moment, good Drivers are concentrating intensely – have the brakes released properly? Is the train moving properly? Is that damn signal still Green? (As strange as this last one sounds, many signals can be replaced to a red or 'Stop' aspect at any moment, not least in some serious safety situation, and Drivers must be continually vigilant for it occurring). If the train is moving normally and no alarms or buzzers have sounded, or warning lights appeared, then you're finally on your way…I think this is a good moment to look at Cab Controls.

Cab Controls

I can't not cover this – it's for the benefit of less knowledgeable readers. For those familiar with train cabs, I'm still not going into detail. I may be an ex-Driver but I still don't intend to make it easy for anyone to steal a train…

Direction Selector

As simple as it sounds. Forward, Neutral and Reverse. Reverse is almost never used on multiple unit trains, except perhaps in depots and maintenance sheds. It is used on locomotives, although still not that often.

Power Handle

This can be a fairly long handle on older locomotives, a shorter handle on more modern locomotives, and a combined power/brake controller on many modern trains. It gets us moving, by having power applied – whether from a diesel engine or electric transformer –

to some form of traction motor, which will basically turn the wheels.

Brake Handle

On a locomotive there are often two of these – one to be used if the locomotive is running without a train and the other, larger one, to be used if there is a train attached to the loco. And, as mentioned above, many modern trains have the brake controls combined with power into a single handle. Just to confuse things, slightly older 'multiple units' will have a power handle but only one brake control (because they always have a train 'attached' as it were).

Emergency Brake

This is often a handle or a plunger. It's a faster way to apply all the available brakes instantly – to do this with the brake handle requires a different physical movement, usually through several brake positions (some brake handles can have 3 positions, others 6). There isn't a huge difference but it's worthwhile. This emergency brake can also be used in a variety of operational situations.

Speedometer

Much like your car. As you can imagine, there are some fairly precise instructions regarding when this thing stops working properly, including usage of your computer screen's digital speed (if you have it).

Brake Gauge

This shows how much pressure is being applied when you make a brake application. On locomotives it can also show a brake 'pipe' pressure, which is used for the 'brake continuity test' we heard about earlier.

Main Air Reservoir Gauge

Shows how much air is in the overall air system. This is obviously critical – a minimum pressure is required to have all systems on the train functioning normally. It was never fun to see this sucker dropping, often agonisingly slowly, and often suggesting a leak somewhere.

AWS Cancel Button

This relates to one of the UK's main safety systems – the 'Automatic Warning System'. All trains have an AWS sensor on the bottom of the leading vehicle or loco. Most signals on the railway line have an 'AWS magnet' around 200m before the signal. That's the whole system. The colour of the signal governs whether the magnet is energised or not. Green or 'Proceed' signals cause a bell or a 'ping' sound in the Driver's cab. Single or double yellow signals cause a loud sound (it's sort of like a honk but it certainly gets your attention) and you then have around 5 or 6 seconds to hit the AWS Cancel Button. If you don't do so then the train's brakes will apply and you will grind to a halt. There's also a visual indication on a small dial in the cab. And yes, just like you're thinking, most Drivers have – at one time or another – managed to not hit the cancel button in time and have their train grind to a halt for no good reason. Hopefully you only ever do it once, as it's recorded on the black box, and your manager will quite rightly start to wonder if you're as alert as you should be…

DRA (Driver's Reminder Appliance)

This is another UK safety system, consisting of a round plastic switch which illuminates red when it's pressed inward. This also has the effect of blocking the power – your train won't move, no matter what you do with the Power handle. It's to be used at very specific times – stopping at a red signal and leaving the cab when another Driver is taking over, being two of the main ones.

It can be particularly useful at station stops where the last signal before the station was showing a caution, with the next signal likely to be red. Performing all the tasks of a station stop mean the Driver can forget that the previous signal was a caution, and the DRA is to be operated anytime after receiving the caution up to stopping at the station. Many red signals were passed this way – usually in an almost identical situation where the first signal after the station would be round a curve and just far enough for the train to have built enough speed to make stopping in time impossible (as we'll see later).

Horn

Such an important piece of kit, you wouldn't believe it. There are strict instructions governing problems with this, as you would expect. Well, what would you do if you'd ignored a problem with it and you round a curve at 80mph to see a trackworker on the rails? Yep, that's why we take it so seriously.

Sanders

As mentioned earlier, pressing this button will deposit sand beneath at least one set of wheels, and is obviously used when struggling for grip. These are now pretty widespread, and not just on old Freight locomotives as you might have thought.

Wipers

Another one that's more important than you would expect. You only need one wiper to stop working perfectly and you can find yourself with little visibility in the rain at high speed…that's no way to run a safe railway. There are regulations for Wiper (and windscreen, obviously) defects too. On modern trains there's often a Washer system incorporated, and if you're lucky there may even be a Demister (which would be another button).

Lights

Headlights, tail lights, other lights. Even on newer trains the headlights don't necessarily show the Driver that much of what's out there, although they're a vast improvement on a few decades ago. There are detailed instructions for defects, yet again. There's obviously some form of internal cab lighting too, which will have its own control.

Communications

On locos this is often some type of radio that allows communication with Signallers, or indeed anyone else on the network whose number you've got. On passenger trains there will be an additional handset for onboard communications with other staff, or indeed to make announcements to passengers should this be required.

Buzzer

These still appear on modern Passenger trains as it's simply a good, concise way for the Driver to communicate with the Guard (and essential if the fancier stuff stops working). A simple 'buzzer code' (such as 3 buzzes, pause, 3 buzzes – Guard or Driver to speak on internal telephone) transmitted by pressing a button in the cab, allows basic communication.

Door Controls

Obviously only on Passenger trains. These open and close the train doors on the entire train.

Pantograph Buttons

Sounds a bit naughty. Wasn't she a character in a 1970's TV show? These are for the large piece of equipment you may have noticed on top of electric trains, which makes contact with the overhead wire and gathers electricity for the transformer on the train. There's usually a button to raise the Pantograph and one to lower it (no, I told you, it's NOT naughty). When trains are shut down overnight or for prolonged periods, the Pantograph may be lowered. There are also operational situations when it may need to come down (that's it, you were warned, go to your room).

So those are the most common controls, certainly on UK trains. There may be additional switches and controls, often safety-related, but the list above is present on the vast majority of trains. Many modern trains have some form of onboard computer – this often means there will be a computer screen in the cab. This usually allows instantaneous displays of faults or messages, as well as allowing the Driver to go into various menus to check train systems. This is incredibly useful. IN THE OLD DAYS Drivers would often have a vague indication of some fault (or none at all), and have to go through a sometimes lengthy process of finding the exact issue before any remedial actions could be taken.

As well as the controls and computer screen, there are numerous fault lights, data recorder lights, safety system lights, door interlock lights (when lit indicating that all doors on the passenger train are closed properly), 'line' light on electric trains (when lit it indicates electricity is being received through the Pantograph – you really don't want to see that light go out) and a bunch of others. Yes, there is a lot to watch over. Not exactly in the 'Pilot league' but a lot more than you'd expect.

7
Let's Talk About Training

There's no avoiding this.

Training isn't just extremely important at the start of a Driver's career, it'll have the same importance until the day he retires. New trains, new signalling equipment, new regulations (often as a result of an accident or incident) and new procedures are introduced continually in the rail industry. As you're at the sharp end of the business, and as your complete understanding of anything 'new' is required to avoid deaths and catastrophic accidents, you're forever going to have to take training seriously.

We can divide Train Driver training into two main areas : initial training and ongoing training. Let's look at each in turn.

Initial Training

There are strict regulations about the minimum required training for Train Drivers. If you're lucky enough to get one of these sought-after jobs, you can look forward to around six months of 'basic' training. This is always a mixture of classroom and practical training. It will cover railway basics such as signalling systems, principles of safe rail operation, basic features of a train, railway safety systems (both on-train and off), basic train driving skills, rail incidents and the regulations to be followed, professionalism (can cover many topics such as alcohol/drugs, sleep quality, communication skills, dealing with distractions and other subjects) and often some basic First Aid and Fire training (this largely consists of which extinguishers to use and which not to use, on different types of fire).

During the basic training, trainees will spend time in train cabs, observing other Drivers and 'acclimatising' themselves. At a certain point, you will go with a more experienced Driver (these have various titles, from 'Instructor' to 'Mentor' to who knows what) who has a qualification in training other staff. You must now start driving!

The Instructor will retain responsibility for the safe working of the train…but you will actually be in the driving seat and driving the thing. Initially, this is every bit as nerve-wracking as it sounds. Depending on the company you have joined, you might find yourself one morning at the controls of a 10-coach Passenger train departing from a major station, or at the controls of a 1000 tonne Freight train leaving a busy freight complex in bad weather. Everyone has to start somewhere…

There are a mandatory minimum number of hours you must physically drive a train during your initial training. This obviously varies in different countries but the concept is the same – to give trainees a good chunk of hours in the driving seat, with an Instructor present to bark "Get that brake on now!" and any other instructions which ensure you don't mess up while still learning.

There is usually some attempt to have trainees drive during darkness too, as this can be quite unsettling to new Drivers. This period of driving with an Instructor will last a good number of weeks, so you should encounter a good variety of weather conditions too. The greater the number of unusual or difficult incidents a trainee encounters in this period, the better. This means they have an Instructor present to answer any questions, and remind them of the regulations to be followed in each scenario.

Of course, there's no way to guarantee what may occur when you're actually out and about. Unfortunately, it's quite possible that you will encounter some serious situation on your first week as a new Driver, and you've only ever discussed it in a classroom. Companies have invested heavily in Train Driving Simulators of varying quality, and much of the time Drivers spend in them will see all kinds of horrors being thrown at them…fires, snowstorms, defective signals, large cows on the track, and basically everything that could possibly occur. The hope is that Drivers who are exposed to these incidents in a Simulator – getting a chance to 'practice' procedures – will be better equipped to cope when they inevitably encounter them in real life. Once again, it's copying the airline industry. And a very good thing too.

"Things That Can Happen While You're Driving A Train"

Another part of the job that is rarely spoken about is the killing of animals. Most common by far are birds, although anything from pet dogs and cats to sheep, stags and more exotic animals can become victims of your train. A lot will depend on what kind of driving you do. Long-distance express Drivers report killing a lot of birds, plus a selection of most other animals (that high-speed stuff can also have a lot of downsides). If you drive slower trains then the carnage will be lessened, but there will still be unavoidable incidents. It isn't talked about often, and I'm not going to go into it in any detail, but every Train Driver has killed a bunch of animals.

If you're an animal lover then it will definitely be one of the worst aspects of the job for you (hitting the brakes on most trains is going to save pretty much none of the wildlife that runs/flies/crawls/whatever out in front of you). What I would say, for the benefit of non-railway people reading this, is that trains are often cautioned for domestic animals being on the line. Railway staff do make an effort to try to get your pets safely off the railway tracks. It's just a fact of life that any animal that makes its way onto the railway is in extreme mortal danger. And let's leave it at that.

Back to our training, and once the 'basic' training is complete, trainees are given some title like 'Qualified

Driver' (they might get a bump in salary at this point too) but there is still a great deal of training to go. At this stage, trainees are likely to split into different areas of training as required by their particular depot. Even within the same company, specific training requirements can be quite different for different depots. If you're going to be based at a small depot out in the countryside, you may only require training on 1 or 2 different types of train or locomotive, and may only need to learn 1 or 2 main routes. But if you're based in a city, you may need to learn 3, 4 or more types of train, and 5 or 6 routes or more.

Learning a single type of train will take around 2 to 3 weeks, but if different trains are simply variations of the first type, then it's usually only a few days to learn the particulars for each subsequent variation. If the different trains are radically different, then longer training will be required. After the training on trains or locomotives is complete, the final hurdle is to learn the different routes.

Route learning is a peculiar business. At first, especially if you've never been on the route before (note that most trainees will have seen the routes in the basic training, but if you transfer location once you're an established Driver it could be totally new), it's simply a matter of asking the Driver's permission to sit in the cab and view the route through the windscreen. A 'pass' may be provided by your Supervisor, which allows the holder to enter the cab for route learning purposes.

After a few days, or perhaps longer if it's a complex or long-distance route, the Driver may offer the route learner the chance to drive. If the learner feels confident enough, he may take the controls. Obviously this is by far the best way to learn a route properly, but there is no rule which states that a route learner must be offered the chance to drive.

The original Driver retains responsibility for the train, and for this reason some Drivers simply do not offer route learners the potentially risky opportunity of driving their train. I always did it, but only after asking a few questions of the route learner (I wouldn't bother if the person had just begun learning the route – it's too soon, and actually counterproductive if they get a fright). Even after allowing a route learner control of the train, I always kept a close eye on them throughout the journey. I wouldn't have been the first Driver to receive disciplinary action for a mistake made by someone else…

Depending on the length of the particular route and its complexity, route learning a single route could take anything from a few days to over a month. And just how do you 'learn' a new route? Well, all countries and companies have publications which contain the details of each route. This will tell you certain basic things for each route, such as the type of signalling system, all speeds, location and layout of junctions, and special instructions (e.g. certain types of train prohibited in certain locations, such as extremely heavy Freight over an old bridge).

Some companies will additionally produce route 'maps' specifically tailored for Drivers, which tend to have a higher level of detail, such as displaying individual signals. This still doesn't tell you what you really need to know – which is braking points. Basically you need to know that if you're approaching 'Happytown' station on a Class 233 train and you're travelling at 100mph, then you need to apply the brakes before you reach that large white house on the hill, on the left-hand side. Or if you're approaching 'Stinksville Freight Sidings' with a 1000 tonne train and you're travelling at 40mph, then you need to begin braking at the old overbridge next to the farm with the giant barn. Yes, this really is how Drivers learn routes.

These trackside features act as general markers for stations or sidings or junctions. Obviously these are treated as 'in ideal weather' – so if it's raining heavily or snow has been affecting the braking of your train, then you will know to start braking even earlier. Of course, the farmer might suddenly demolish his giant barn, and the white house might suddenly be painted green. As a Driver you usually find that the locations become 'automatic' braking points fairly quickly, and any changes to landmarks thereafter can be taken in your stride.

The other main aspect of route learning is to find out any 'tricky' areas on the route. Bizarre as it may sound, the proximity of a nearby factory may make braking in that immediate area quite tricky (this could be due to any number of fumes or outputs from the factory which end up affecting the rails). All of these things are learned and remembered while route learning.

If your company doesn't provide maps, some Drivers take their own notebooks and write down major features themselves. There may even be 'route learning videos' available in your company's training facility. These can be extremely useful for refreshing your memory of a route, particularly ones which you don't use very often. Your depot may require you to sign several 'diversionary' routes – these are routes of varying lengths which are used when there is a problem on the main route. So if a train ahead of you grinds to a halt with a major technical issue, the Signaller can reroute you onto the diversionary route and the journey can continue. Assuming, of course, that you haven't already passed the junction for the diversion. If you have, then you're in for a long wait. Due to the fact that you may go many months between journeys on these diversions, companies have systems in place to track when a Driver may need to 'refresh' these routes. This may involve travelling in the cab of a service which uses the route, viewing videos of the route, or both. Route 'knowledge' of all kinds must be kept up to date.

"Things That Can Happen While You're Driving A Train"

Flooding can mean anything from a few inches of standing water which never actually reaches the rail, to torrents of water which can close the line for several days. The big worry from a railway standpoint is that moving water can actually begin to move the ballast (the piles of small stones which hold sleepers and therefore the track in place) and this can mean that rails are liable to bend as trains move over them. This may result in the derailing of either that particular train or the next one to come along. If you're wondering 'Wouldn't the next Driver see the bent rail and stop?' I can tell you that most of my encounters with flooding happened during darkness. Depending on the type of train you're driving, you may not have a great headlight and may not be able to see that well, particularly in bad weather. Not fun.

Even worse is when ballast is moved away at the site of a culvert. This generally means a pipe or small passageway (anything from a foot to several feet in diameter) which has been run under the track, usually buried several feet down and emerging from a banking at each side. When the ballast has gone (and for several reasons it's quite likely to be washed away at a culvert) the tracks are usually suspended in mid-air, and are in no state to take the weight of a train travelling at speed.

There's not a lot to be done when you encounter flooding, except follow the regulations in regard to reporting it and driving through it. Jokes about 'wellie boots' and diving suits are optional when speaking to your colleagues onboard.

Once you've learned all the initial routes required by your depot, and signed in a folder to say you're competent to work them, that's it! You've actually completed your initial training and will now become an everyday, productive Driver at your depot. So let's now look at ongoing training.

Ongoing Training

Obviously if your company orders a new type of train then you will require training on it. This will happen at some point, but years tend to pass before new trains appear.

Drivers receive publications – these include company manuals but also publications on general railway regulations, routes, and other technical matters. These publications will be updated on a continuous basis. Some will receive updates every couple of months, while some may only be updated after several years (though with these there tend to be mini-updates sent out in the meantime, which Drivers have to learn anyway). In all cases, Drivers are legally required to read and learn the contents of these updates – in their own time (which often means while sitting waiting on a train somewhere). All of these processes are becoming simpler as the industry uses more electronics like tablets and smartphones, but paper manuals and notices are still in use.

"Only On The Railway?"

One of the oddities of driving trains is that you pass a lot of your colleagues going the other way throughout your working day. The number of colleagues will vary, as a Freight Driver working in mostly remote areas will see a limited number of other trains. A suburban Driver however, will be passing colleagues every few minutes. Some Drivers wave at the Driver coming the other way. Some Drivers only wave at Drivers who work for the same company. Other Drivers only wave in response to a colleague's wave. And some Drivers never wave at all.

I never did figure out the etiquette while I was working. The subject was rarely brought up, with a wide spectrum of feelings on the matter. Some of my old colleagues said "I don't even look at the cab coming the other way" and some, like moody teenagers, took the huff when other Drivers didn't wave back. I heard that in the UK, at one point, they were looking at introducing a rule to ban waving at oncoming trains because it was a distraction to both Drivers. As far as I know, it never happened. What a strange, strange job it is...

Proper training courses only tend to happen for something major. For example, in the UK there was a move towards using in-cab telephones, linked to the mobile phone network, to facilitate communication between Drivers and Signallers. Instead of you getting out of the train and bumbling along the trackside in horizontal rain and 60mph winds to an old telephone on a signal, you could make a call to the Signaller without leaving your seat (and you're more likely to be able to hear him without the blasts of wind, passing trains, rain bouncing off everything, and other helpful ambient sounds). The operation of this new system was complex, so most companies organised training over several days with an Instructor, in order that all Drivers would be on the same page.

So ongoing training is a combination of small-scale self-training and larger, less-frequent training courses.

One thing's for sure, training is a hugely important part of your job, and it never ends.

8
Driving Part One

Back to our early morning cab. We're leaving the station and the journey is underway...You'll be having a quick glance at your gauges and warning lights just to make sure everything's fine. And a Driver's eye never wanders from the Speedometer for too long...

The start of a journey is always the twitchiest time for a Driver. Not only are you still 'feeling' the health of your train (if you brought it empty from the depot to a station you may have travelled at anything from 5 to 30mph, now you may be travelling at anything up to 100mph or more) but if you've departed from a major station or Freight yard, you are still likely to be in an area filled with other trains/complex signalling/junctions and other potential hazards. Concentration will be particularly intense. If non-railway readers are thinking "Well, so what if anything goes wrong at this early stage? How bad could it be?", I think we should have a look at the Ladbroke Grove crash in the UK.

Ladbroke Grove

On October 5th, 1999, a 3-coach Class 165 Passenger train left Paddington station in London. At the controls was a young Driver who had only recently qualified. Around 5 minutes later, 31 people were dead and 523 injured. The Driver had passed a red signal shortly after leaving the station, and his train collided with an incoming express service.

This momentous accident resulted in huge changes to Train Driver training and many safety processes in the UK rail industry. A Government inquiry investigated all aspects of the accident and made extensive recommendations. Links to the full report can be found here : https://www.railwaysarchive.co.uk/eventsummary.php?eventID=142 .

I don't want to go into too much detail, as this was a complex accident where multiple factors contributed to the passing of the red signal and the horrendous consequences. For our purposes, one of the key factors was that the Driver's training had been inadequate, in respect of both his route learning and his approach to dealing with red signals. In addition, the signal he passed at red had been passed at red on numerous previous occasions by other Drivers. Extensive information and discussion on these matters can be found in the official report.

The key point is this : a young, newly-qualified Driver made a mistake. Given all the circumstances outlined in the official report, it wasn't that hard a mistake to make at that time. And just look at the outcome.

Thanks to the detailed recommendations of the accident report and many years' hard work by safety professionals, engineers, train designers, management, unions, training staff and those on the frontline, such an accident is simply not going to happen again. Newly-qualified Drivers are now substantially better trained than in 1999, and are assessed much more closely and diligently. Signalling is better designed, better installed, and inspected more carefully than in 1999. Consequences of errors are considered more carefully in designing track layouts than in 1999. Signallers are trained to react more quickly to SPADs than in 1999. All in all, the industry has done a very creditable job in tackling the issues identified in the report. Hopefully this is the smallest of comforts to those who lost family or friends that day.

I hope that if you take nothing else away from this book, you'll appreciate the heavy responsibility that most Drivers have. These big machines take a long time to stop, even if you slam the brakes into Emergency. The consequences of Train Driver mistakes can be very serious. That's just the nature of the job.

Depending on the route, you may soon emerge from the outskirts of the station into open countryside. If you work city services you may spend your entire shifts either within the city or in suburbs. Even though you may drive mainly 'local' services, the term 'local' could still cover a lot of ground. In the same city, Drivers at different depots could work intensive city services at one depot, while Drivers at the other reach the far outer suburbs or adjacent towns.

The intensive city work could easily involve over 100 station stops per shift, while those lucky enough to be doing more suburban work could have around 50% less stops. In short, the variety is huge. If you work for a long-distance Passenger company then the routes tend to be less varied (although you will travel further on them, at higher speeds). Freight companies, in the UK at least, use the same routes as Passenger companies, although there are many Freight-only branches to factories and other organisations.

Let's take two of the commonest types of Train Driving as examples : intensive city Passenger work and long-distance Passenger work.

Intensive City Work

Everything we've spoken about up to this point is fairly similar, in terms of going to depots, getting your train and working it empty to the starting station (the other way to start your shift, particularly later in the day, is to relieve another Driver – so you may hop in a taxi at the depot to go to the station and await the arrival of your colleague). However, the actual services you work may be very different depending on your employer and location, so once the journey begins the job can become quite different. Intensive city work generally means two things – a smaller train and a lot of station stops.

This kind of shift means powering the train up to a relatively low speed (you may rarely get above 30/40mph) then almost immediately getting the brakes on for your next station stop. It's often possible on city networks, as a member of the public, to see the next station stop along the tracks, just several hundred yards away. This is not necessarily the most satisfying type of train driving, but it is incredibly demanding. An argument can be made that this type of driving is in fact more challenging than the long-distance work, which tends to get the higher salary and the glamour.

Another factor of intensive city work is the level of aggravation. These short-hop services attract fare-dodgers and feckless humans of every kind (partly because it's impossible to dodge fares on many buses now), particularly in the evenings and at weekends. Therefore you know when working these services that there's a probability of disruption. This could be anything from abusive passengers who vanish before any police arrive (after refusing to leave the train for 10 straight minutes), to having multiple windows smashed by stone-throwing vandals and the cancellation of your train. The more dramatic stuff obviously happens less often, and all of these events also take place on long-distance trains to a lesser extent, but city work is always going to include this type of unnecessary aggravation.

"Things That Can Happen While You're Driving A Train"

One of the more unusual 'city' situations related to me involved a Driver who was braking his train into an inner-city station. This station had a footbridge going across the track, with stairs leading down onto each platform. After stopping his train, which happened to have its stopping point at the foot of one of the staircases, he glanced across at the opposite platform and saw a gentleman sitting on the stairs, wearing a shirt. And nothing else. I understand it wasn't a particularly long shirt either. The gentleman was just sitting, gazing peacefully across the station.

The Driver reported this immediately – not only was there the possibility of children arriving at the station (luckily I believe the place was pretty much deserted), but the situation didn't bode well for the mental health of the man in question, and there were infrequent 'express' services which passed through that station at more than enough speed for anyone with a suicidal tendency. Drivers tend to have gallows humour (we'll come back to the dark side of the job later) so this story caused a fair bit of mirth, but most of us were probably also thinking to ourselves that it was fortunate this incident didn't develop into anything more problematic. And no – as far as I know no-one heard the ultimate end to this story, which might well have been the local Police dragging the man off to the local cells for either a talking to, or some charges. The saddest part of the story is that the station in question was in a particularly poor and crime-ridden part of that city, so that a man sitting on the station stairs dressed only in a shirt wasn't as big a deal as you might imagine.

Alternatively, one of the upsides to 'city' work is that you are indeed mingling with the public more than usual. These multi-stop runs can only go on for so long (Drivers' mental concentration has to be taken into account by train company planners) so after less than an hour (although it can be longer) you are often given a short break. This could be anything from 5 to 25 minutes ('official' breaks as mandated by law are strategically placed in Driver's shifts and usually 30 minutes long as a minimum, but it varies) and might only allow you enough time to change cabs from one end to the other on a multiple unit.

But it will allow you a brief respite, perhaps a chance to go to the bathroom on your train (and by that I mean use the on-train toilet, you people…), and maybe even have a quick chat with colleagues or members of the public. Contrast this with long-distance Passenger Drivers or Freight Drivers, who may be stuck in their cabs for 3 hours or more without a break.

Slightly removed from the intensive inner city work are those routes involving the outer suburbs and perhaps beyond. Working these services tends to mean fewer stops and perhaps a bit more countryside. You're still not likely to get the train speed up particularly high, but the fact of simply getting to let the train run without braking for prolonged periods is a tonic if you've worked a lot of inner city services previously.

"Things That Can Happen While You're Driving A Train"

Members of the public who go onto railway tracks are crazy. It's true Russian Roulette. You don't know when the next train is due and you can't be sure what speed it's travelling at. Even if you'd memorised the timetable there are can be late-running, or many occasions when a locomotive or empty train may be sent out without warning. Why would anyone ever take such a chance? Some of the biggest scares I had in my driving career were caused by people being on the track when they shouldn't have been there. Sometimes it's members of the public, and sometimes it's trackworkers who have broken some rules in order to try to get their work finished on time.

It's one of the worst parts of being a Driver (along with slaughtering all kinds of wildlife as you thunder along the track, unable to stop or deviate). Those last few seconds as you approach the person or persons...with the brake already smashed into the 'Emergency' position and still travelling at high speed...and you're starting to brace yourself for a horrible impact...and you're watching them, hoping that they're going to get out of the way just in time...

Of course, there are also people who go on the tracks with the specific intention of not getting out of the way. Sadly, suicides are a part of Train Driving. There's nothing you can do to prepare for it – just hope you're one of the lucky majority who never have it happen. Drivers react in all kinds of ways. Some are back driving trains within a few weeks. Some are off work with psychological issues for many months. At the extreme end of that scale are Drivers who never drive a train again, and even Drivers who take their own lives after such an incident. Thankfully the latter scenario is incredibly rare, but anyone considering a career as a Train Driver needs to realise suicides are potentially a part of the job.

Inevitably, as with emergency personnel and medical staff, some Drivers cope with black humour. One Driver I was told about would occasionally relate the grisly details of a fatality (when he felt it was appropriate, obviously). He'd been driving a locomotive with one of those large metal coupling hooks at the front. I believe it may have been a passenger service he was hauling, and some unfortunate man walked out in front of the train, which was travelling at some speed. This man, in fact, had stood so centrally between the rails that he had inadvertently lined himself up perfectly with the coupling hook.

When the Driver got the train stopped and went down to check the front of the train, looking for possible damage and expecting the unfortunate man to be way back down the track, he found him impaled on the hook. As he would tell this story (so I'm told), listeners would invariably ask the question that's going through your head at this moment. Yes, the unfortunate man was dead. But the Driver would then go on to relate that when emergency responders arrived at the scene, they had to at least make an attempt to revive the man. "But," he would relate with a wicked grin, "They couldn't get him off the hook. It took ages. They were trying all sorts of equipment - railway stuff, anything they could find - to lever this guy off the front."

Knowing Drivers as I do, I don't think for one second this guy was anything other than traumatised at the time this originally happened. I don't doubt he had the utmost respect for the poor person who decided to end their life. And I'd bet major money that a few years passed before he was able to relate this story with any kind of morbid grin. Maybe this was his only way to cope with such a terrible incident in the long term.

From Drivers I've personally come across who've had this type of experience, I can only say that there are as many different stories of coping mechanisms as there are people. No-one can say how they would react until it happens. Thankfully, most companies now offer much better care to Drivers who undergo these experiences. Many Drivers complete a long career without it ever happening to them. So to anyone considering Train Driving as a career, don't let this dark side of the profession put you off – it isn't likely to happen to you.

IN THE OLD DAYS depots structured the routes in a manner that meant the really awful, unpleasant work was done by the new and younger Drivers. Older Drivers would be rostered in so-called 'links' which contained a lot of the best quality work. It worked like this….say your depot had 80 Drivers. There might be work over 3 routes which was regarded as 'good' – either because it had few station stops and/or the services didn't start very early or finish very late.

There might also be different work over 2 other routes which everyone hated – again, it could be because of vast numbers of station stops and/or extremely early or extremely late services. In addition to the main routes, there are also odd shifts involving things like empty train movements or even shifts where you simply move trains around the depot as required (many companies have this done, or intend to have this done by depot employees, by training them to drive trains at very low speed in depots).

The depot management, in consultation with unions, might split the work into 2 links of 40 Drivers each. This split used to be done on the basis of 'seniority'. So the first Driver allocated to 'Link 1' would be the longest-serving Driver, followed by the next longest-serving, and so on. Of course, this means all the new Drivers will be shoved into the end of 'Link 2'. The next step would see Link 1 being allocated all the shifts with what was regarded as 'good' work. This could be all the work over the 3 supposed 'good' routes, or just most of it.

Some depots (if the older Drivers were really decent guys) would allow a sprinkling of 'good' work to go to the 'junior' men, but not always. Link 2 would usually have all the work regarded as just 'not-so-great'. Because in those days it could be years before a railway employee was promoted to a Driver's post, the newly anointed Drivers were usually so pleased just to be driving at all that they didn't complain much about the Link situation.

You can see the logic in this – the older Drivers considered that they'd 'done their time' working the horrible stuff when they were younger, and wanted the easier stuff now that they were getting a bit creaky. And the theory was that the junior men, through gradual retrials/quitting/deaths/transfers of older Drivers, would eventually find themselves moving to Link 1 and the better work. This all became problematic when the European Union brought in employment legislation to combat 'ageism'. As far as I know, the rail industry continues to dance around the issue of 'seniority' to this day.

Anyway…on to the other stuff.

Long-Distance Passenger Work

In contrast to 'intensive city work', long-distance Passenger work can be summarised as : longer trains and few stops. In fact, some depots have routes where a Driver can drive for over an hour before making a station stop. There may only be 3, 4 or 5 stops on the outward trip and possibly even fewer on the return. So…a possible total of 8 station stops in an entire shift, as compared to our previous city example with well over 100. The speed tends to be considerably higher – in the UK up to 125mph for prolonged periods. Quite a contrast.

Despite the differences with intensive city work, the key to performing properly remains the same : concentration. It's obviously a little easier to let your attention wander if you're out in the countryside, with long straight sections of track, and with no station stop due in the next 30 minutes. Although you may be driving at 125mph, it's unsettling just how quickly Drivers can become accustomed to these speeds. Some modern trains have what is effectively a 'cruise control', which adds to the potential for concentration slipping (although it can be argued that it also lessens fatigue, because the Driver isn't continually fiddling with controls to maintain a constant speed).

One of the key things about driving these faster trains is to be able to react quickly to events. The consequences of incidents at high speed are generally more serious. This is presumably the thinking behind the tendency for rail companies to pay these Drivers higher wages. Again, the argument can be made that the Driver doing intensive inner city work, making over 100 stops a day, is subjected to more opportunities for a catastrophic error – possibly resulting in fatalities. And the counter argument is that accidents at 30mph will kill far less people than those at 125mph. Also, long-distance trains tend to carry a lot more passengers – that's a lot more bad PR if you start killing them, if you'll excuse the bluntness. Yet the chances of an incident are simply higher in busy, complex city network situations. You can see how this discussion could go on forever…

"Things That Can Happen While You're Driving A Train"

As we saw with Ladroke Grove and Chatsworth, passing a red signal can be catastrophic. Even without fatalities or damaged trains, passing a red – often by just a few feet or a few yards - is a disaster for the Driver. It's the big bogeyman of a Driver's career. It will be on your record for a prolonged period (depending on country) and is always likely to be in the back of your mind whenever pressure situations occur. I was lucky to never have one, and always felt tremendously sorry for those who did. It was a massive blow to their professional pride as Drivers. And there are so many ways it can happen.

I heard horror stories where a Driver was distracted at a critical moment, usually for good or innocent reasons, and the result was a SPAD (Signal Passed At Danger – the terminology used by safety experts in the UK). One involved a Driver stopping at a station en route to his destination. He'd received a single yellow signal just before the station, meaning the next signal would be red. But the next signal was round a curve and wasn't visible from the station. As soon as the Driver stopped his train he had a lady knock on his cab window to ask questions about train services at that station. He should have activated his DRA switch, which could have reminded him of the red signal. But, according to the story I was told, the knock on the window came almost at the instant he stopped, distracting him from his DRA. Apparently the lady continued to ask questions throughout the station stop, and having made a real effort to answer the numerous questions, the Driver suddenly found the Guard giving the buzzes to proceed. As a result of the conversation, all memory of the previous yellow signal was gone. He accelerated the train, rounded the curve and couldn't stop in time upon seeing the red signal. Because of the location and time of day, there was never any possibility of a major incident, as is the case with the vast majority of SPADs. The Driver would have been formally disciplined, although I never heard what happened to him.

No Driver ever passes a red signal intentionally – at least none that I ever heard of in my career. There's a good reason for this : the Driver is at the business end of things, and will be the first to die if there's a collision. Aside from that, it's a matter of your livelihood and professional pride. Pass more than one red signal – particularly if the incidents are only a few months or a year apart - and your company will be taking a long, hard look at you and wondering if you've got the right stuff. I'm not aware of what the current regulations would be for these situations, but I can't imagine you'd be left at the controls of a train for long if it looks like you're not up to the job. Even without the possibility of losing your job, professional pride dictates that you should do everything you can not to cause a SPAD. It sounds easy when I write that, but I can't tell you how many times I thought, after hearing the details of another Driver's SPAD, 'There but for blind luck go I.' SPAD stories are almost always a 'perfect storm' where several factors come together at a particular time, and these can undo the best of Drivers.

Fortunately for Drivers, the rail companies have put huge effort into SPAD research and investigation over many years. This means Drivers receive more training, assessment and information than in the past. There is much more awareness of the issue and, certainly towards the end of my career, I saw much more effort to help Drivers tackle the factors which can lead to SPADs. While it remains the bogeyman of professional Driving, SPADs - particularly ones with disastrous consequences - are much less likely today, given the efforts of the rail industry and its staff.

Back to long-distance work, and one of the peculiarities of it is the requirement for a healthy bladder. The inner city work tends to have more opportunities for a Driver to pay a quick visit to the bathroom (whether on his own train or at a station). Long-distance can require a Driver to drive continuously for over 3 hours before there's a possibility for a bathroom break. There may be a few station stops but these tend to be incredibly rushed at best, and there's every chance you might zoom along to the nearest on-train toilet and it's occupied. It's not something you'd immediately think about, but if you have any kind of bladder dysfunction then long-distance or freight train driving is probably not for you. I know that many Drivers have used an empty soft drink bottle when the situation has required it. It seems to me this kind of emergency measure is more suited to freight work, where you are entirely alone on the train. On long-distance Passenger work there is always the possibility the Guard will enter your cab quite suddenly – for any number of reasons – and that could be problematic…

In terms of driving skills, the basics are the same. You will simply be braking from further out as you approach a station (because you're going faster). Long-distance companies tend to have better trains – better in terms of performance. So not only is it likely to accelerate away from a station more quickly, but the brakes will probably be more effective too. These things make staying on time a lot easier. If you factor in the bonus of coffee/tea/snacks which will sometimes be offered by on-train colleagues, these long-distance Drivers really can have a pretty good time of it.

"Railway Matters"

One of the unquestionable positives to being a Train Driver is the exposure to sights of natural beauty. If you're lucky, at least some of your routes may take you through outstandingly beautiful countryside. Even if you're mainly a suburban Driver, some of your driving will expose you to cityscapes or other impressive vistas. Even if there is no spectacular natural scenery, you will be seeing the world at very early and very late hours. Both extremely early sunrises and very late sunsets in Summer can be beautiful, regardless of your location. Other natural phenomena, such as harvest moons, meteor showers, or the Northern Lights, may only be glimpsed because your job placed you in a particular place at a particular time.

Many Drivers enjoy seeing all the seasons played out in routes they drive over again and again. Millions of office workers around the world would love to have the sense of freedom and even, perhaps, adventure that Train Drivers experience on a daily basis. I'm not sure they'd want the hours, though. Anyway, whether you're a nature lover or not, it's a strange human being that isn't moved by seeing spectacular natural beauty. Or perhaps a city skyline on a June morning at 0400. Tick this one in the 'Pro' column.

IN THE OLD DAYS the long-distance Passenger work would have been in the top link at a depot. It was regarded as the most attractive work even then. This also ensured that it was the most experienced Drivers at the depot who were working high-speed trains with hundreds of people on them. Today it's possible for a member of the public to join a rail company, undergo their training courses of approximately a year, and find themselves on their first day at the controls of a very fast train with hundreds of passengers. At Ladbroke Grove, training was a factor in the incident (although that Driver wasn't employed by a long-distance company), and all rail companies - in the UK at least - have made substantial improvements to their Driver training. In the 20 or so years since that disaster, no major incidents have occurred as a result of inadequate training of Drivers.

Now that you have an overview of city and long-distance work, we should talk about the mid-point of your shift. On long-distance this is approximately when you'll have your longest break. This may also be true on some city work but those shifts tend to be a lot more fractured and disjointed. A long-distance Driver may do just two trips of 3 hours each, from point A to point B and then back, while city work will involve multiple trips of varying lengths to various destinations. As we're looking at a typical working day, let's look at the arrival at first destination, which will approximately correspond to the first long 'break' in city work.

9
Arriving Part One

It's always nice to arrive at your first destination. Whether you've just done 3 hours of continuous high-speed driving and need a rest, or you've completed the first of several city trips after many station stops, the first part of your shift is done. We'll assume you're now going to have your first break, although the city shift is often likely to see you do some more trips before that happens.

"Things That Can Happen While You're Driving A Train"

Depending on your country and company, you will have mandatory 'ride alongs' where a company manager will sit in the cab for a certain length of time. They must observe you doing your job properly. Later they will write a report and this will count as one of your regular 'assessments'. Another regular assessment would be a random download of a data recorder of a train you've driven. In addition to these, an exam on your knowledge of rules and regulations would be held at regular intervals (anywhere from every second year to once every five – there is huge variation in different countries). If you're really (un?)lucky there may even be a 'simulator' session to undergo every few years, where all manner of incidents like a fire, broken rail, animals on the line etc. may be thrown at you.

These assessments are all unnerving to a certain degree. I never got used to them and never felt particularly confident (although people will tell you that's exactly how a good Driver should feel). I was lucky with the managers I worked under – they were all a pretty decent and fair bunch. That's certainly not always the case, as with any organisation. Still, even if you know the manager sitting across from you in the cab is a decent guy, you know he's still watching every move you make. Once you're more experienced there tends to be a bit of chat on these occasions, which always helps. At least if you make a mistake (hopefully minor), you are able to instantly explain how you managed to do so. Alternatively, it got a bit awkward when a manager asked you about something on a data recorder download from three weeks previously, when you barely remembered that week, never mind anything more specific.

On long-distance you'll stop the train at the stopping point and release the doors so your passengers can get out. In the UK the stopping points are marked by numbered boards on platforms, which either show where to stop with a certain number of coaches ('4 Car Stop'), or where to stop with a particular 'Class' of traction ('Class 222 Stop'). Drivers learn these on Route Learning.

Usually on long-distance work there will be another Driver waiting to take over your train, which may only be half-way to its destination. City trains may see this situation too, but they are more likely to be 'terminating'. This simply means they've reached journey's end. This may be a dead-end on a city branch line, or simply a particular station where trains often terminate for operational reasons (often a station where different tracks meet).

If you're handing over to another Driver you must tell him about any issues which could affect the working of the train – "The brakes are isolated on the third vehicle. Control are aware. Speed is limited to 90mph" and similar. Most often the train is fine, and you might simply find yourself explaining why you've arrived a few minutes late. There's never much time on these handovers, whatever the situation.

It's worth saying that it's not always fun taking over from another Driver. If you work for a large company and you travel between major cities, then you may not see the same particular Driver from another location again for months. Although a certain shift has you handing over a specific train to Drivers from a certain depot, that depot may have over 100 Drivers and you may only do that shift semi-regularly. This can be the only explanation for the fact that some Drivers, despite the knowledge that they're going to be handing over the train mid-journey, leave the cab looking like there's been a crazed party of some kind. Litter, food remnants, stains, smells…all the fun of the fair. I can honestly say I never did this personally, and it was always a puzzle to me when other Drivers did so.

"Things That Can Happen While You're Driving A Train"

One hair-raising incident I was told of (third-hand, but I heard other similar stories from that area) concerned a small, local train. This was a suburban service which travelled just outside a major city, and it reached speeds of around 75mph on certain parts of the route. On a dark evening, the Driver had stopped at one of the earliest stations on the route, which had a slightly curved platform. Apparently Drivers had to exercise extra care on this platform to ensure no passengers were trapped in doors, before departing. The station was deserted at this particular time of night. The Driver had arrived early at this station, so had relaxed in his cab for a moment in order to wait for the correct departure time.

When ready, he glanced back along the train and was confused, as he thought he saw movement at the very end of the train. Not at the last door – where any passenger might have been – but at the very back of the train. He looked back for several seconds but saw nothing. He began to wonder about just how tired he was. He then operated the button to close the doors. Deciding he must have seen a bird flying past the rear of the train, and not wanting to cause delay, he moved the power controller to the lowest power position and the train began to move very slowly.

Still troubled, he looked back along the train as it began to move and saw the unmistakable head of a youth pop out from the back of the train – that is, he appeared to be on the <u>outside</u> of the back of the train. The Driver immediately brought the train to a halt. The youth jumped onto the platform and sprinted out the nearest exit.

There was a small 'step' on each end of this particular type of train, which was designed to help maintenance staff undertake certain repairs. This youth must have thought it would be fun to stand on it, and presumably hang on for dear life to the next station (which was about 10 mins away). This apparently happened over 25 years ago. So...an early 'trainsurfer' before the internet made it commonplace. Luckily for him that Driver was paying enough attention to save him from his own stupidity.

If you're terminating the train then it's a matter of opening the doors for your passengers, changing the destination and the lights on the front of the train, and shutting down the controls. On intensive city shifts you may have ten minutes or less to walk to the other end of the train and get it ready for departure. Unless mandatory breaks are required, this is the most efficient way to work these services. If you're a few minutes late and in need of bladder relief, there will be a rush to reach the nearest toilet and hope it's not occupied. If you're working a long train it can take quite a few minutes to reach the other end, and open up the driving controls.

There's two ways to look at situations like this. Firstly, and the industry would offer this one to the media, there's a 'safety' issue regarding a Driver trying to concentrate when his bladder is the size of a bowling ball. The rail companies would always tell the media that the Driver should go to the bathroom, delaying the train if necessary. I know of few Drivers who did this.

The reason virtually no-one does it is because you would have to explain the delay to your manager (which could be a costly delay for your company if the industry has a 'fines for delay' system, as in the UK). Do it a few times and you might find yourself being sent for a medical to determine if you had "bladder issues" incompatible with your profession. Now, again, I know of no Driver who has been sent for a medical after delaying his train for a pee (NOTE: Trains do not pee.) Drivers can be a paranoid bunch, but with good reason. So the reluctance to delay trains for a Driver toilet break is huge. The only cases I personally heard of, where Drivers had delayed trains due to being in the toilet, involved diarrhoea. As mentioned before, a weak bladder and Train Driving do not go well together.

So the city Driver is probably driving another train fairly soon after his first arrival. At a certain point in the shift though, he will be due a mandatory break. The long-distance Drivers often have this break after the first arrival. Let's have a closer look.

The Mandatory Break

Firstly, depending on the driving content of a shift, you may have one break of around 45mins towards the middle of the shift, or two breaks of 30mins approximately spaced out at certain points in the shift. These are approximations of UK guidelines, which are agreed with rail unions and are changed every so often. The overall aim is to give Drivers a useful break or breaks, relevant to the particular shift in question.

As well as stipulated time points in a shift, breaks must occur in a location where Drivers have access to some kind of cooking equipment, a sink, and a toilet. Even these requirements may be up for 'negotiation' with unions. In the UK, rail companies have for many years been trying to get agreement for Drivers to take their 'break' on board actual trains. Fortunately, most union officials have resisted this move. Driving is actually a reasonably stressful job, requiring prolonged periods of mental concentration and alertness, and, if you're doing a 100-plus stopper in a city area, a surprising amount of physical work. Therefore, the thought of having your 'break' on a busy, noisy train, wearing full uniform, is not appealing. In the UK, unions have largely insisted on breaks 'away from the railway environment', as they've always been.

Even 'facilities' can be dramatically different, depending on the company and location. The best facilities – usually in a room at the station as far from the public as possible (for noise purposes) – can have relatively new and comfortable furniture, sometimes a television, and clean cooking and sink areas. If the room is used by enough people there may even be vending machines. At the other end of the scale, with facilities used by few people or in remote areas, there may be some worn chairs and a table, a grubby sink, and a microwave and kettle that have seen better days. There may not even be windows. These are the places where many Drivers spend their "break", sometimes in the company of colleagues or staff from other companies, but possibly alone. Don't become a Train Driver if you want to work with people throughout your working day…it's a solitary profession, sometimes even out of the cab.

Drivers, being human beings, also find lots of ways to pass the time on their "break". If the station where the break is scheduled is in a city, then there are no rules to stop you wandering out to browse the shops or buy a decent cup of coffee. Obviously the length of your break is crucial here, as you may be called back to the station quite suddenly after the mandatory minimum period of the break is over. This doesn't happen often, but companies quite reasonably expect you to be 'available' given that you're still on the clock. Telling your manager that you didn't hear the phone in your pocket because of the noise in the shop you were in, doesn't go down well.

Other Drivers go for a walk, some actually go to the gym (again, with one ear on the phone), and some have even been known to get on another train and take a short hop somewhere else. The truth is, the more adventurous activities mentioned here are only feasible on very long breaks indeed, and depending on the company you work for you may never actually have a break long enough – and/or in a relevant place - to ever do them.

Many Drivers just remain in the staff area to eat some food and talk with colleagues. Some remain in the staff area and read a book (although it's rarely a quiet locale), and others produce headphones and watch material on their phones or whatever other electronic device they choose to bring with them. Often there are other grades of staff in these break areas, and this can be helpful in fostering more of a team approach, and to get the conversation off driving (although some Drivers minimise the 'shop' talk on their break).

With the regulations on mobile phones, many Drivers spend the first few minutes of their break listening to voicemail messages and responding, firstly on the company phone and then on your own. Most days the company won't have called you, but depending on how long your phone's been off, the personal one usually requires some attention. This is something non-driving staff on trains have no conception of – they will have been using their phones throughout the journey (discreetly). As a Driver, especially if you only have the minimum break time in that particular shift, the switched off mobile phone can cost you a less than ideal chunk of your supposed break to sort out. It's a pain, but as Chatsworth proved, those phones simply have to be off when you're in the driving cab, however long that may be.

There are as many ways to use the break as there are Drivers. The key element is that you are rested from your driving activities, eat and/or drink as necessary, and take a proper bathroom break. You should be in good shape to return to the platform or freight yard or wherever else, and do the next piece of driving.

"Things That Can Happen While You're Driving A Train"

One of the times you really earn your salary is during 'degraded' working. This has different terminology in different countries, but basically means a time when the normal signalling systems are not in operation. There are obviously very strict rules for such situations, but this doesn't necessarily make things easier. If high winds have caused issues with the overhead power cables and/or signalling then you may have multiple areas of concern to concentrate on.

Although you will often be travelling at reduced speed, there are many points to remember from your training, as well as keeping a constant watch on changing circumstances around you and your train. Usually the training for these circumstances is very good, but being trained, even in a simulator, and experiencing the real thing are very different propositions. And you may have been trained many months or even a year or more previously, and suddenly without warning you're placed in the real situation.

Everyone ends that first experience soaked in sweat, muscles and fingers aching from clenching controls, but hopefully a bit wiser and battle-hardened. The next time that situation erupts in your nice, quiet working day you will only be 90% as freaked out as you were that first time. And so it will continue, until eventually your freak-outs are minor and your experience is substantial. That's the job.

10

Driving Part Two

If you're on a long-distance job then your shift may be half over, and the remainder of it will concern you getting back to where you came from. Sometimes the shift may be slightly more complex, and involve three destinations with three trips. Whatever the case, you have to end up where you started. In terms of the city work, you may have anywhere from 5 to 10 or more separate journeys of varying lengths. At some point, however, you'll be on your last journey of the shift. On Freight, some companies have Drivers do a long, one-way trip. If there are no passenger services to get them home, some companies have taken to hiring vehicles. So some Freight Drivers may find themselves driving vans almost as often as trains.

"Railway Matters"

Hands up those readers who have watched video compilations on the internet of trains ploughing through road vehicles on level crossings? Quite enjoyable from a distance, huh? Sometimes you see the vehicle occupant jumping out and getting a safe distance away. What you never see is the poor Train Driver who has smashed the brakes into 'Emergency', is blasting away on the horn, is possibly stood up ready to jump for it if required, and is hoarsely muttering a string of curse words. He or she is calculating as best they can, in a very short period of time, just how bad things might get.

If you're the Driver of a huge freight train and you're crushing a small family car which is clearly empty, then the stress level is going to be around 'high' ("Man, what a mess this is going to be. I hope none of the air pipes on my locomotive are damaged too badly.") If you're the Driver of a local passenger service and you're screeching towards a large tanker truck, then the stress level is going to be 'stratospheric' ("Sh*t! That could be milk or it could be fuel! I can't tell from this angle! I'll be the first to die, then my passengers in the front coach...")

The level of danger around all level crossings is such that any railway employee cannot conceive of anyone with half a brain taking a chance around them. The equipment at different types of crossings is always designed to protect both the road and rail users. Things get crazy when people stop obeying the instructions.

Next time you see one of those level crossing disaster videos, spare a thought for the key participant you never see - the Train Driver. Did I mention you can't have a weak heart if you're a Train Driver? Well, I'm mentioning it again.

Your train comes in to the station – hopefully on time – and you wait for the Driver to jump out. The words you want to hear from him are something along the lines of

"Everything's fine." What you absolutely don't want to hear is that there is some obscure technical issue with the train which could worsen as your journey continues. This happens more often than any of us would like. It's particularly stressful if it's a fault you haven't encountered before. Faults on trains and fixing them constitute an important part of the Driver's role. Let's take a look.

Faults and Fixing Them

IN THE OLD DAYS, Drivers were trained about the workings of their locomotives or trains to a very detailed degree. Because of the way the promotion system used to work, future Drivers could find themselves waiting years to become a fully-fledged Driver. Although most Drivers (but not all), would actually allow you to drive the train in order to gain experience, it could be extremely frustrating and also unhelpful to your family finances to wait so long. The major upside to this situation is that you would be exposed to all the potential mishaps, weird situations, and rare incidents that the railway could throw at you. And the Driver you were with was always in charge, so - no pressure, man.

In the modern industry, the several months that trainees spend driving trains with an experienced Instructor present, is supposed to take the place of the old 'extended apprenticeship'. But the experience gained is invariably less. Hence the very real possibility that, as a newly appointed Driver, you find yourself taking over a train with a fault which you dimly remember being mentioned just once in the distant past of your training. What do you do?

As trains have become more complex and expensive, there has been a tendency among train companies to reduce the leeway which Drivers have to actively go and tinker with their assets (behave yourself). The preferred method is to call a maintenance number which is staffed 24/7. Someone is paid to sit at a computer, with access to all kinds of manuals, software, fault-finding charts and who knows what else. The procedure for the Driver is to basically tell them what's going on and do whatever they tell you.

Some companies are providing tablets which contain a certain amount of fault-finding information, but the 'guy on the end of a phone' makes sense in the majority of situations. Of course, if the fault occurs while you are actually driving a train then you'll be calling up another staff member on the internal comms and requesting that they do the phoning for you. If you're alone on a train, whether it be empty coaches or freight, then you'll have to use your training and judgement to decide when and where to stop the train so that you can address the fault. And make the telephone call.

In the UK, the regulations have become ever more complex as to what faults require you to stop and when; and who to report them to. This largely came about as the industry introduced more and more financial penalties for delays to trains. Increasingly, Drivers in that country do NOT want to be the one stopping a train in a position where it blocks a major line. Thousands of pounds or more can be racked up in a few minutes spent phoning, only to find out that you needn't have stopped the train for that particular fault. And the flipside to that is the Driver continues on with a fault he should've stopped for and some incident occurs, for example passing a red signal. Faults can be damn tricky.

If you're lucky enough to be driving one of the very modern trains then there's a good chance you'll have a nice computer screen in your cab. This screen will usually helpfully tell you exactly where a fault is, and often what to do about it. Of course, you can have a fault with this computer or screen too – aren't you lucky? Small exterior bodyside lights can also be used as guide to the Driver for the locating of faults. And of course there are the obvious signs of a fault like smoke, heat, or various noises like air escaping or metal grinding. But if you have one of those computers with fault-finding capability then your job is an awful lot easier. If you're in a freight company or simply working an older passenger train, then you'll have to do a lot more of the investigating yourself.

Fixing faults, and they are fixable in the majority of cases, can involve anything from flicking a circuit breaker just behind your Driver's seat, to crawling underneath the train to operate a well-hidden lever that hasn't been used in months. What everyone is trying to avoid is a 'failure' situation. This is when the Driver has to basically give up on fixing the problem and ask to be rescued. Obviously this is a lengthy, tricky and disruptive process, and everyone hates it – the Drivers, the onboard staff, the passengers, the Signallers. Another train has to be located, one which is compatible in terms of coupling up to the 'failed' train, and which is as geographically close as possible (this still might be 45mins away or longer). This 'rescue' train will itself be delayed, so that's a second train of passengers inconvenienced. So, as you can imagine, the railway likes to avoid 'failures' as much as possible.

To keep trains rolling, even with faults on important equipment like brakes or safety devices, the rules in the UK often allow Drivers to keep going but usually at a reduced speed. These regulations are continually modified to avoid 'failures' without compromising safety. This can be a difficult process. In 1997, at Southall in England, 7 passengers died and 139 were injured as a result of the Driver's lack of attention to signals. However, an important safety system had been isolated, and due to financial considerations the former requirement to have two Drivers present in trains travelling at over 110mph had been removed. Despite this shifting of total responsibility to one Driver on high speed trains, no modifications were made to the rules governing situations where Drivers lost important onboard safety systems.

The lone Driver had been preparing his bag for leaving the train at journey's end, and managed to miss not one but two warning signals. But the isolated safety system would have provided him with an additional alert to those warning signals. He couldn't stop at the red signal and smashed into a freight train which was crossing to another track. The rules were subsequently changed so that when that safety system was isolated, another member of staff was required to ride in the cab with the Driver to ensure that he was reacting to warning signals. Nobody wants trains frequently cancelled or 'failed' with faults, but nobody wants multiple deaths either. That's the tightrope those unfortunate people who draft the railway rules are always walking…

Anyway, spare a thought next time you're sitting on a delayed train with a 'technical fault'. Your Driver may well be crawling about below one of the vehicles, trying to find and pull a disgusting dirt-encrusted handle, which the maintenance staff on the phone *swear* will make everything okay…

Hopefully your ride home is fault-free. The return journey will either be the same route in the opposite direction, or if you're on a shift with 'triangular working' (which is a three-journey shift with a second destination on the middle journey – think of it like a triangle with the journeys being A to B, B to C, and finally C to A, so you get home!) then you have a bit of variety and will have three different routes. The run back always felt less demanding to me (unless something went wrong, of course) as you were, at all times, on your way home. This doesn't mean I relaxed in any way – that would be potentially dangerous for a Train Driver – but it was psychologically less of a burden than driving further away from home with each turn of the wheels. In a similar vein, regardless of the time of day you started your shift, you're likely to be that little bit more tired than earlier. Being aware of this fact always helped me to make an effort to keep my concentration levels up on the journeys home.

"Things That Can Happen While You're Driving A Train"

Drivers are often 'cautioned' by Signallers. This means you will be stopped at a signal (or you could be contacted during a station stop) and warned by the Signaller that there is something ahead of you that you need to be aware of. This could be animals, trespassing humans, faults with signals/track/level crossings, or some more outlandish ones. I've heard of Drivers cautioned because pieces of equipment have fallen from maintenance vehicles, or lineside engineering equipment has fallen onto the track. Drivers are sometimes asked to stop and remove such items, as stopping multiple trains and warning their Drivers soon leads to large delays.

In the UK, swans are a special case. Most of our winged friends end up as a bloody mess somewhere on the front of the train (sometimes stuck under a wiper for an hour or more while you try to dislodge the gory remnants), but swans who wander onto the railway require trains to be cautioned and driven at slow speed. Some poor trackworker or local track manager is then called up and made to pursue this exceptional ex-dinosaur until he somehow gets it away from the track. You can probably imagine someone who joined the railway with a great interest in engineering, staggering along the track, possibly getting pecked at..."I didn't sign up for this, dammit!"

Another factor in this part of the working day is that you've already done several hours' driving. Any rustiness or cobwebs should have been well and truly removed by this point. This doesn't mean your driving will be super-smooth and faultless but the likelihood of making really dumb minor mistakes – the kind that happen when you're just back after a week on vacation – is much reduced.

As well as a happier Driver, I noticed that the Guards often tended to be a lot calmer on the way home. Like everyone in a job, once you pass the halfway point of your working day everything seems a bit less of a chore. The only thing about return journeys, particularly if they go to a terminal station, is that passengers start fretting about making their onward connections. This can make the end of the Guard's shift a lot more involved and stressful than it might have been, especially if you're working a late train and people are trying to catch the last trains of the day to their final destination. On the whole, however, the journey home simply feels more enjoyable than the earlier ones.

"Things That Can Happen While You're Driving A Train"

One of the parts of the job I particularly disliked was driving through a station I didn't stop at, at high speed. The possibilities for things to go wrong were too great. Having said that, nothing ever did. But it's just plain uncomfortable hurtling towards a platform where you can see groups of people (or even children) messing about just a few feet from the platform edge. Even if people are at least the minimum distance away from that edge, they tend to move about and worry you.

And there are those delightful people – most of whom seem to be boys aged around 13 to 18 – who think it's funny to make a sudden move towards the edge as you approach. Oh yes, Drivers find that hilarious. It's particularly unfunny for those Drivers who've actually had someone throw themselves in front of their train at a platform (this happened to a colleague at one of the companies I worked at, his train was travelling at over 100mph). I'm not sure there's anything to be done about these situations beyond the measures currently in place. I can only say I'm very glad I don't have to do it anymore, and that all those sphincter-clenching moments weren't, as luck would have it, foretelling some horrendous incident.

11

Arriving Part Two

This is usually a good part of the shift – the main work's done. It's always a good feeling approaching your final destination of the day. So many things can happen on the railway, from the comic to the horrific. Every time you complete a shift without either a screwup, lengthy delays, or anything else unwelcome, it's a good day.

As you make the final approach to the platform, it's the same feeling you had in the last 5 minutes of the school day. Having said that, this is also one of those times you really need to stay focused – you're at the end of a shift, when you may be mentally and physically tired, and you may also be ending it at a buffer stop on a busy platform in a complex station layout. Lots and lots of opportunities for things to go wrong. You stay focused and get the work finished.

"Only On The Railway?"

A strange thing that seems to occur in various countries is the presence of aircraft over a train. What is it about pilots – whether they're plane or helicopter, military or private – that draws them to trains on the ground? I've heard multiple stories over the years of Drivers, always in the countryside of course, realising that a helicopter or plane is either following their train along part of the route or repeatedly passing them. Drivers often joked (perhaps accurately, who knows) that some of the military aircraft were probably locking on to their trains as some kind of target practice. More likely is that the pilots were having a bit of fun. Another strange railway-related phenomenon that few people will have heard of...

Once you have stopped the train at your final destination and opened the doors, your only remaining duty is to ready the train for the next Driver. This means adjusting the lights so that only red tail lights are on at your end (assuming we're in a terminal platform and your driving cab is going to be the rear of the next service), adjusting any destination indicator (if indeed you know the next destination), and finally closing down the driving desk and removing your key. In terms of driving, you're finished!

Sometimes you may actually meet the Driver who is taking over the train for the next service. This allows you to tell him about any difficulties you may have had – although you will have entered any faults into the Maintenance Repair Book in the cab, and possibly phoned in to the Maintenance desk as well. Indeed, this would be the last thing – if required – before leaving your train. Any good Driver taking over a train will usually check the Maintenance Repair Book to see if he's going to have a carefree or problematic start to his journey.

"Things That Can Happen While You're Driving A Train"

Snow is fun! Everyone loves snow, right? Snow is not fun for Train Drivers. Okay, maybe if you're having a brief snowball fight with colleagues in the car park at the depot. But snow has probably made your trip to work a bit of a nightmare. And it doesn't end there. Because most modern trains don't like snow. In the UK, there have been years of ridicule in the media over snow. 'Why' is a bit of a mystery. It's simply technical issues, which are not easily overcome when you are designing fleets of trains to operate in mostly mild weather.

I believe in the UK one of the main problems is that fine, powdery snow gets into parts of trains you don't want it to, and causes problems. The trouble is that you can't seal up the underside of your train to keep out this powdery snow, because then the equipment under the train will overheat the rest of the year. No easy solutions, and the UK media could learn these simple facts if it really bothered.

The truth, as railway professionals know, is that it's a minor miracle that so many trains actually do run on time to their destination. It's a complex undertaking, unless you're on a very simplistic network with only one or two different train types. Which isn't a description of most of the railways of the world...

After you've shut down the train and spoken to colleagues, you now only have to return to your depot. How you do this will be on your schedule. But that's the serious 'work' part of the shift over. There will be a spring in your step. Unless the shift was a horror story with all kinds of complications. In which case you'll be trudging off, hoping that nothing else can go wrong before you reach the depot.

12

Back To The Depot

There are three main ways to get back to your depot (assuming you aren't based in the station). Taxi, riding on an empty train, or walking. You'll be pretty lucky if you can walk back to the depot, and this often refers to Freight Drivers who are based very close to the Freight yard where their journey finishes. Riding on an empty train tends to happen in the evening and beyond, when trains are returning to the depot for the night. Many other Drivers will require a taxi.

It can be very frustrating, at the end of a long shift, to have to wait a long time for a taxi. Hilariously enough, the times when you are most likely to wait are often also the times you have just finished a difficult and/or extended shift. The same disruption after a major fault or incident, which caused your train to be delayed or diverted, usually affects taxis as well. Hordes of inconvenienced passengers may have been placing a strain on taxi services long before you began to wait for yours. That's the job, man.

"Railway Matters"

As often happens on the railway, having expended a lot of time and effort in replacing steam trains with diesel and electric, we have seen them return to action many years later. Dragged out of all kinds of hibernation or 'enthusiast' railways, and lovingly restored to spectacular condition, they now operate on the same main lines that they were removed from decades ago.

From a Driver's viewpoint, many were glad to move on to diesel or electric locomotives, simply because they had a proper enclosed work environment where they could control the temperature. And not have rain or snow coming at them at varying amounts of speed. Working on a steam footplate was a serious business. Not only was there a great deal more physical work - firemen shovelled tons of coal per shift while the Driver had to use a lot more muscle power on the various controls - but there was coal dust, smoke, the occasional blast of flame from blowbacks, and a lot more concentration required to keep those beasts working optimally.

Some Drivers missed the steam trains, saying that the job had been 'de-skilled'. It had, but a different skillset was required for the diesels and electrics. Drivers who volunteered for the reintroduced steam trains, who had no previous experience, were apparently very impressed with both the skill required and the physical demands of the job. In fact, older Drivers, who could be a bit portly, used to joke that they had had the body of an athlete before the industry took the steam trains away and stuck them on a modern locomotive "Sitting on my rear end all day". There were often two groups of these older men, among those who had actually worked steam trains on an everyday basis 'back in the day'. One group genuinely missed the skill and unique experience of working them. The other group would claim to be glad to see the end of them, as their daily working environment had improved tremendously.

All these Drivers, however, would agree that the steam locomotives were fabulous machines. If you haven't seen one working in real life, I recommend you do so.

The taxi to the depot is also another opportunity to report any issues to the Maintenance desk, if your call didn't get through earlier. If your train was delayed in a lengthy or unusual manner you may also want to ring your company's Control office, so that they are aware of exactly what happened. It's worth doing it at the time, otherwise your manager may get a call or an email the following day and come looking for you to get an explanation. By which time you may well have forgotten. Or was I just getting old?

Rolling into the depot in your taxi at the end of a shift is definitely a good feeling. But you're not quite finished yet.

13

End of Shift

Almost done!

Inside the depot, once you've deposited your equipment in your locker, you will go back to the admin room to see if you have any mail in your mail slot. You also need to check the shifts for tomorrow, in case yours has been altered in any way. These duties are usually in your manual and your contract, so they shouldn't be shirked. This is also a final chance to fill out any necessary paperwork pertaining to the day's shift. This could be a report about something that happened, or a form concerning a signalling issue. Again, these are all laid down in the regulations and your contract, so they're mandatory and not just 'good practice'.

"Railway Matters"

As with all jobs, if you're a Train Driver for any length of time then you will come across quite a range of characters. From fellow Drivers to Guards to catering staff to platform staff to ticket office staff to managers to office staff to engineering staff to Signallers to members of the travelling public, you're going to meet an incredible range of people. Some of them will make you proud to be human. Some of them will make you wonder how they were ever employed (these characters tend not to last). Some of them will become true friends. Some of them will annoy the hell out of you.

I'm not sure the rail industry is a special case, but it certainly has a spectacularly wide range of characters working in it. All my best memories are related to particular people. They made me laugh, or made a nice comment, or helped when I was struggling. I was lucky to be trained and mentored by people who were very professional and were good at their jobs. I hope I gave a similar impression to newer colleagues in later years. It's a heavy responsibility, this Train Driver business, but it's also an unusual and rewarding career. Whether you realise it or not, it's about the people. Always was. Always will be.

If there are colleagues around the depot you will probably have a chat, though these tend to be quite brief at the end of a long shift.

And that's it. Hopefully you got a bunch of people or a load of freight to their destinations safely. You head for your car in the car park. All you have to do now is drive yourself home safely.

14

Home

If you've had a very long shift with incidents or bad weather or whatever else, you really want an uneventful trip home. That's the thing, next time you're sitting in rush-hour traffic at 1730, you might keep in mind that the man or lady in the queue next to you – who look like they're ready to strangle someone – may be a Train Driver who should have been home three hours ago and needs to be in bed pretty soon for the next day's shift.

Once home, you will try to spend some quality time with your significant other. Assuming they're not also a shiftworker, in which case you may not see them in any meaningful sense for a few days. It's worth saying once again that Train Driving will take a toll on your personal life. Hopefully you're with someone who understands and helps you cope with all the problems it can bring.

On the upside, you are bringing home a good salary which should provide a good quality of life for the occasions when you can actually spend time together. And spending time apart can be healthy – I had plenty of colleagues who thought the shiftwork provided 'space' for both them and their partners to actually have a better relationship than if they'd both been in 9 to 5 jobs. No doubt it will come down to the individuals involved.

You may have domestic things needing done, or to get things organised for tomorrow, or you may just want to sit and relax for a bit.

But…depending on the exact shift you have the next day, and just how long and tiring today's one has been, you might not actually have all that much time before you need to go to bed and start it all over again.

That's the job. That's what Train Drivers do.

Afterword

I hope this has been an enjoyable and enlightening read for you.

Train Driving, even in the 21st century, still has some mystery about it. There's nothing wrong with that, and this book certainly hasn't revealed all the details of a Driver's job – you'll only find those out by doing it. But I hope reading this book means you'll have more of an appreciation for those mostly-hidden figures who are only occasionally glimpsed on station platforms.

It's a tough job, whatever company you work for. Drivers are expected to maintain concentration for prolonged periods, no matter how unnatural the hour, no matter how long they've been on duty, no matter how many days in a row they've been working. The consequences of dropping your guard for even a moment can be fatal. There aren't many jobs like it.

J Smith,

July, 2019.

If you enjoyed this book, please leave a review at the website where you purchased it. Just a few words are required, and would be much appreciated. Thank you.

If you wish to receive information on future Railhead Publishing releases and free samples from them, please submit your email address to :
https://mailchi.mp/eae804e4b852/railheadpublishing

Please note that your email address will never be shared in any way, and will only be used for the purposes stated above.

Printed in Great Britain
by Amazon